The Absolute Best

DUMP CAKE

COOKBOOK

The Absolute Best Dump Cake Cookbook
Quick Start Guide

HUNGRY?
TURN TO PAGE 51 FOR CHOCOLATE CHIP

ON A DIET?
TURN TO PAGE 76 FOR FAT-FREE ANGEL FOOD PINEAPPLE

GOING TO A POTLUCK?
TURN TO PAGE 62 FOR CARAMEL APPLE

WANT TO IMPRESS YOUR FRIENDS?
TURN TO PAGE 37 FOR BLACKBERRY-MERLOT

THE ABSOLUTE BEST

DUMP CAKE

COOKBOOK

More Than 60 *Tasty Dump Cakes*

ROCKRIDGE
PRESS

Contents

1

....

Dump That Cake!

DUMP CAKE DOESN'T SOUND very appetizing, but it is actually a delicious dessert that is so named because the ingredients are "dumped" into a pan and then baked. This type of cake has gone by a variety of names over the 100 years since the first known recipe was published. Depending on where you live, your area may have its own name for this type of cake, such as "wacky cake," "crazy cake" "hole-in-the-middle cake" or "cockeyed cake."

Early dump cake recipes called for flour, baking soda, and other dry ingredients, but when boxed cake mixes hit the grocery store shelves in the 1930s, home cooks were ready to make their baking as effortless as possible.

Recipes for "crazy cake" made with boxed cake mixes were first publicized around 1937, and they continued to gain popularity from there. This easy dessert was renamed "dump cake" in a 1980 baking pamphlet put out by Duncan Hines that featured recipes using their cake mixes.

A dump cake recipe can be as simple as a box of cake mix, a can of fruit, and a stick of butter, or it can be as complex as a combination of fresh fruit, homemade cake mix, butter, nuts, and other ingredients. It's up to you. Don't be afraid to create your own versions of dump cake!

Why We Love Dump Cakes

Americans love dump cakes primarily because they are so delicious. Besides, there really is no other cake that is easier to make. A box of cake mix, some fruit, and a little butter are all that you need for a basic dump cake recipe. No measuring, no mixing, no complicated cooking techniques—this cake is so easy a five-year-old could make it with very little help. The basic instructions for preparing a dump cake are as follows:

1. Preheat the oven.
2. Grease a baking pan.
3. Spread a can of fruit in the pan.
4. Pour the cake mix over the top.
5. Pour in the melted butter.
6. Bake.

That's all there is to it. It's mixed right in the pan you use to bake it, so there's no fussing with measurements and, best of all, no cleanup!

Given the simplicity of a dump cake recipe, you might think that they are all the same, but that is not the case. Using different flavors of cake mix, different fruit, and different flavorings are just a few ways that you can create infinite variety with this dessert. Most of the recipes you will find for dump cake, however, start with one of the following four flavors:

* White cake
* Yellow cake
* Chocolate cake
* Spice cake

That doesn't mean you can't substitute another flavor to create your own variations. These boxed cake mix flavors are simply a place to start—let your imagination soar with the rest of the ingredients! Combine different fruits, flavors, and add-ins to fulfill your own flavor fantasies.

10 Tips for Making a Great Dump Cake

No matter how delicious or how easy a recipe is, there are always ways to make it better or easier. Here are ten tips to help you make blue-ribbon dump cakes:

1. Always use unsalted butter, especially if you are using a commercial cake mix. Most boxed cake mixes contain a lot of sodium already, so you don't need to add more from the butter.

2. Do not use margarine, whipped butter, vegetable shortening, or oil in place of the butter, because it simply doesn't work as well.

3. Do not stir the ingredients unless the recipe specifically calls for it. The ingredients for dump cakes are meant to be added in the order listed. There are exceptions, however. Once you have gained some experience with making dump cakes, you can make the following changes to adjust the texture to your liking: If you briefly stir the ingredients together before baking, you will have a moist cake with fruit on the bottom. If you don't stir the ingredients at all, you will be left with something similar to a fruit crumble or crisp.

4. If you don't have a chocolate or spice cake mix on hand, you can make your own by adding ingredients to a yellow or white cake mix. Just add 5 tablespoons unsweetened cocoa powder for a chocolate cake. For a spice cake, add 1 teaspoon ground cinnamon, $\frac{1}{2}$ teaspoon ground nutmeg, $\frac{1}{4}$ teaspoon ground ginger, and $\frac{1}{4}$ teaspoon ground cloves. You may also want to throw in a pinch of chipotle chile powder.

5. When a recipe calls for adding canned fruit to a dump cake, canned pie filling works best because it is already thickened and doesn't make the cake too wet.

6. Any dump cake can be made gluten-free by using a gluten-free cake mix. Make sure to check the other ingredients for gluten as well and make substitutions as needed.

7. Reduce the fat in your dump cake recipe by leaving out the butter and covering the top of the baking pan tightly with aluminum foil. The cake will steam in the oven, staying tender and moist without the added fat.

8. To make a dump cake recipe even easier, you can cook it in the microwave. You'll just need a pudding-type cake mix, 3 eggs, and a can of pie filling. Mix the ingredients in a 3-quart microwave-safe bowl and then microwave on high for 13 minutes. After cooking, cover the bowl and let the cake cool for 5 minutes. This cooking method will work with almost any of the recipes in this book.

9. You can also make dump cake in a slow cooker. Simply grease the inside of the crockery insert with cooking spray before adding your ingredients. Spread the fruit in the bottom of the insert first and then sprinkle the cake mix over the fruit. Drop pieces of butter over the mix and cook on low for about 3 hours.

10. If you are making dump cake in a slow cooker, consider lining the crockery insert with parchment paper to keep the edges of the cake from overcooking.

Recommended Ingredients

Even though the recipes in this book are short and sweet, it is important to use high-quality ingredients to achieve the best results. Here are some tips to help you create drool-worthy dump cakes every time.

CAKE MIX

Nearly every recipe in this book calls for a box of cake mix. If you spend any time at all in the baking aisle at your local grocery store, you will see that boxed cake mixes are not all the same size. At one point, boxed cake mixes were all about 18.25 ounces, but the three biggest cake mix manufacturers downsized their cake mixes. To further confuse things, these three manufacturers didn't all downsize the same way. Some cake mixes are now 15.25 ounces, while others are 16.25 ounces. Still others have stayed with the original 18.25-ounce size. You can see how this might be a problem.

Luckily, dump cake is very forgiving. Small differences in the size of your boxed cake mix usually won't be reflected in the final product. However, if you want to follow the recipe exactly, you can add 7 tablespoons all-purpose flour to a 16.25-ounce cake mix or $10\frac{1}{2}$ tablespoons all-purpose flour to a 15.25-ounce cake mix. (If you have a food scale, you can weigh the additional flour in ounces to be more exact.) To see whether it truly makes a difference, you may want to try making one recipe twice, adding the extra flour the second time.

Keep in mind that you can use any box of cake mix as long as it is around 18.25 ounces. You don't have to add the extra flour unless you really want to. Keep it easy!

NOTE: If you are using a homemade cake mix (see Chapter 7), then you'll use 2¼ to 2½ cups cake mix in any recipe that calls for a 18.25-ounce box.

FRUIT FILLING

Many of the recipes in this book call for canned pie filling. This is a thickened, sweetened fruit mixture that is ready to use in pies and other recipes. A can of pie filling is generally 21 ounces—this is the intended size of the canned pie filling called for in these recipes.

If you'd rather use canned fruit (not pie filling), fresh fruit, or frozen fruit, you can do that as well. Follow the tips below to substitute for 2 cans of pie filling:

* Canned fruit in juice: Use a 29-ounce can plus a 15-ounce can of fruit in juice. Pour the fruit into the baking pan, juice and all, and proceed with the recipe.

* Fresh fruit: Use about 3 pounds fresh fruit and sweeten with sugar to taste. Let the fruit and sugar stand for 15 minutes so that the fruit releases its juice. You won't need any extra liquid—simply proceed with the recipe as directed.

* Frozen fruit: Use 4 cups frozen fruit (as a rule of thumb, 10 ounces frozen fruit equals 1 cup). Treat frozen fruit like fresh fruit in the recipe, sweetening it with sugar to taste before baking.

OTHER INGREDIENTS

Numerous other ingredients can be used in dump cake recipes to add flavor and texture to the finished product. Some ingredients you will find used in the recipes in this book include:

* Nuts: Pecans and walnuts can be exchanged measure for measure. Macadamia or chopped Brazil nuts work well in dump cakes that call for pineapple, coconut, and other tropical ingredients. Peanuts and cashews go well with chocolate.

* Dried fruit: Dried cranberries, raisins, and other dried fruit can be added as desired. Dried fruit is especially delicious in spice cake versions of dump cake.

* Coconut: Sweetened flaked coconut can be added to the cake mix or the fruit, or sprinkled on top of the cake. Toast it or not, whatever you prefer.

* Chocolate chips: Bittersweet chocolate chips add the richest flavor to your dump cake, but any type you prefer will work.

* Toppings: Dump cakes are rich and moist, so they are not typically frosted. These cakes are especially nice, however, when served with a scoop of ice cream or a dollop of whipped cream.

Indulge Your Health

Dessert is an indulgence, not something you are meant to eat every day. This being the case, you can afford to splurge a little in your diet once in a while. If you need to watch your sugar and fat consumption, or if you just prefer to keep these ingredients out of your diet, here are some substitutions you can make:

* Choose sugar-free cake mixes or make homemade cake mix using your favorite sugar-free sweetener.
* Use canned fruit in juice rather than in syrup.
* Use gluten-free cake mix.
* Use your favorite whole-grain cake mix from a natural food store.
* Use fresh or unsweetened frozen fruit and add sugar-free sweetener to taste.
* Halve the amount of butter in the recipe to reduce the fat content. Don't substitute oil unless it's organic coconut oil.
* For a fat-free version, omit the butter and cover the baking pan tightly with aluminum foil. If the fruit doesn't seem juicy enough, add 2 tablespoons or so of fruit juice or ginger ale.
* Extra liquid is generally required for this cooking method to steam the cake while keeping it moist.

Serving Ideas

Dump cake is delicious and easy to make, but it is not beautiful. It is a delectable, comforting dessert that probably isn't going to show up on any five-star restaurant menus. That's not to say, however, that you can't make it appealing and attractive. Try these ideas:

* Scoop the finished caked into a shallow bowl rather than serving it from the baking pan.

- Dust the top of the cake with ground cinnamon or nutmeg.
- For chocolate dump cakes, add a generous dollop of whipped cream to the top and dust it with cocoa powder.
- Give your dump cake a classic presentation with whipped cream and a sprinkling of chopped nuts.
- Scatter chocolate chips, nuts, or coconut over the top of the cake before baking.
- Drizzle caramel or chocolate syrup in stripes over a dessert plate and carefully scoop the cake on top.
- Serve dump cake warm with vanilla ice cream on top. Drizzle caramel or hot fudge sauce over the ice cream.

FLOURISHES MAKE IT EXTRA SPECIAL

A dump cake is an easy dessert to bring to a holiday potluck or party. It even works for birthdays! Here are some ideas to use when serving dump cake for a special occasion:

- Coarsely chop candy canes and scatter the pieces over the top of the dump cake.
- If the cake isn't stable enough on top to hold candles, use stemmed maraschino cherries to hold them. Slit the top of each cherry just enough to poke a candle into it and push the cherry into the cake.
- For a pretty autumn presentation, add whipped cream and then dust the cake with ground cinnamon. You can also go the extra mile by carefully balancing a candy pumpkin on top.
- To decorate holiday cakes, use conversation hearts for Valentine's Day, marshmallow bunnies for Easter, candy corn for Halloween, and candy canes for Christmas.

Now that you are a dump cake expert, it's time to choose a recipe and create something special for your family and friends! Always read the recipe all the way through and check out any tips before you begin.

2

American Classics

WHEN YOU THINK OF CLASSIC American desserts, you will probably find yourself dreaming of apple pie and banana splits. The dump cake recipes in this chapter mimic those timeless favorites in the easiest form possible. These recipes require virtually no preparation and very little, if any, cleanup. Choose from Florida-themed Key Lime Dump Cake or a cake made with the flavors of ripe Georgia peaches, and everything in between.

Children of almost any age can help with the preparation of these dump cakes. The littlest ones can sprinkle the cake mix over the fruit, older kids can spoon fruit out of the cans, and children over the age of eight can easily make these cakes themselves—with adult supervision, of course. Desserts are always a good way to introduce children to cooking and baking. Let them experiment with different pie fillings and cake flavors to come up with their own unique creations.

You never know when you may need a last-minute dessert, so you would do well to keep some dump cake ingredients on hand. Keep a couple of cans of pie filling and a few of boxes of cake mix on your pantry shelf and you'll be able to put together a delicious home-made dessert in no time. Just tell people it's your super-power.

APPLE

Yield: 12 servings Prep Time: 5 minutes Bake Time: 1 hour

What looks like a cake but tastes like one of Mom's warm apple pies? This apple dump cake!

Something between a cobbler and a crisp, this easy dump cake is full of fruit and buttery goodness. The generous filling gives you plenty of plump, juicy apples in each bite and the yellow cake makes a sweet crust that is both tender and crumbly at the same time.

If you want to use fresh apples, it's best to use Granny Smith, Macintosh, Honey Crisp, or other firm, baking apples. You'll get the best flavor by mixing two or three varieties of apples, as each gives its own unique flavor to the cake. Peel, core, and slice the apples, and then add white or brown sugar to taste.

Serve this cake warm with a scoop of vanilla ice cream.

· ·

2 (21-ounce) cans apple pie filling (or 4 pounds fresh apples, peeled, cored, and sliced)

1 box yellow cake mix

¾ cup unsalted butter, melted

· ·

1. Preheat the oven to 350°F and grease a 13-by-9-inch baking pan.

2. Spread the apple pie filling in the bottom of the pan.

3. Top with the cake mix.

4. Pour the melted butter over the cake mix.

5. Bake until the top is golden-brown and the apples are bubbling, about 1 hour.

TIP: If you'd like, you can add ¼ cup raisins or dried cranberries to the filling as well. You might try soaking the dried fruit in rum or brandy for 30 minutes, draining them, and then stirring them into the filling. This changes the texture of the dried fruit and adds a new layer of flavor. If you are using fresh apples, you don't even need to drain the dried fruit before adding it.

PEACH COBBLER

DUMP CAKE

Yield: 12 servings   Prep Time: 5 minutes   Bake Time: 50 minutes

There is nothing better than a big pan of warm peach cobbler bursting with ripe and juicy fruit. It's tough to refrain from tasting it before it's cooled enough to keep you from blistering the roof of your mouth.

You can create a lot of variations of this recipe by using different cake mixes. For example, a butter pecan cake mix is absolutely fantastic when used in place of yellow cake. French vanilla is another delicious option, yielding a cake with a delectable peaches-and-cream flavor.

Any type of canned peaches will work for this recipe as long as they are canned in some sort of liquid. If you are watching your calories, use peaches canned in natural juice rather than heavy syrup, and switch the cake mix for a sugar-free cake mix. Cut the amount of butter in half and you've created a luscious, low-calorie dessert. You can even leave the butter out completely—just cover the pan tightly with aluminum foil before baking.

1 (29-ounce) can sliced peaches in juice (or 3½ pounds fresh peaches, peeled, pitted, and sliced)

1 box yellow cake mix

½ cup unsalted butter, melted

1. Preheat the oven to 350°F and grease a 13-by-9-inch baking pan.

2. Pour the peaches into the pan, along with the juice, and spread evenly.

3. Top with the cake mix.

4. Pour the melted butter over the cake mix.

5. Bake until the top is golden brown, about 50 minutes.

FRESH CHERRY COBBLER

DUMP CAKE

Yield: 12 servings Prep Time: 5 minutes Bake Time: 30–40 minutes

Light, crispy topping covers mounds of ripe, red cherries, adding sweetness and texture to this old-fashioned favorite. Using fresh fruit makes it less syrupy than many other dump cakes that call for canned pie filling.

Always taste your fresh fruit and add the least amount of sugar necessary to make it sweet enough for dessert—too much sugar will detract from the fresh fruit flavor. If you think you were a little too generous with the sugar, adding a tablespoon or two of lemon juice will bring that fresh taste right back.

Choose sweet cherries with a deep red color when they are in season. If you prefer a tarter flavor, Queen Anne cherries are a good choice. You can even mix the two for a deeper, more complex cherry flavor.

4½ pounds fresh sweet cherries, pitted (or two 21-ounce cans cherry pie filling)

1 box cherry chip cake mix

¾ cup unsalted butter, melted

1. Preheat the oven to 350°F and grease a 13-by-9-inch baking pan.
2. Spread the cherries in the bottom of the baking pan.
3. Top with the cake mix.
4. Pour the melted butter over the cake mix.
5. Bake until the top is golden and the fruit is bubbly, 30 to 40 minutes.

TIP: Cherries and almonds are delicious together. Try drizzling 1 tablespoon Amaretto almond liqueur over the cherries before adding the cake mix, and then scatter sliced almonds on top before baking.

SLOW COOKER
DUMP CAKE

Yield: 12 servings Prep Time: 5 minutes Cook Time: 5 hours

Peaches and bourbon complement each other beautifully in this recipe, but if you prefer to keep it alcohol-free, you can easily substitute water for the bourbon. The topping has a different texture than conventionally baked dump cakes—it is a little moister on the top.

Making a dump cake in a slow cooker means that you can run errands all afternoon and have dessert ready at dinnertime. You can use any kind of fruit pie filling and your favorite cake mix in this recipe with no other changes. If your slow cooker is smaller than 4 quarts, lengthen the cooking time by about 2 hours. If your slow cooker is larger, adjust the cooking time accordingly.

Serve the cake warm with whipped cream or ice cream.

2 (21-ounce) cans peach pie filling (or 4 pounds fresh peaches, peeled, pitted, and sliced)

1 box yellow cake mix

½ cup unsalted butter, melted

1 tablespoon bourbon

1. Spray the crockery insert of a 4-quart slow cooker with cooking spray.

2. Spread the peach pie filling in the bottom of the slow cooker.

3. Combine the cake mix, melted butter, and bourbon in a bowl, and stir just until the dry ingredients are moistened—it will be crumbly.

4. Spoon the cake mixture evenly over the filling.

5. Cover and cook on low for 5 hours.

6. Uncover and cook for 30 minutes more.

> TIP: Spiced heavy cream is delicious when served over warm cobblers like this one. Add 1 tablespoon sugar to ½ cup heavy cream along with a few drops of pure vanilla extract and a pinch of ground nutmeg. Spoon the dump cake into a bowl and pour a little of the cream over the top to serve.

PINEAPPLE-CHERRY
·················· DUMP CAKE ··················

Yield: 12 servings Prep Time: 5 minutes Bake Time: 30–40 minutes

Crushed pineapple and sweet cherry pie filling mix right in the baking pan to create a tutti-frutti flavor that your whole family will love. The topping is buttery sweet and just a little crisp, while the cherry and pineapple give the cake a faint tropical flavor. If you prefer a less sweet cake, use light cherry pie filling or a sugar-free variety.

Other fruit combinations will also work for this recipe. Try apple and blueberry, peach and mango, or apple and cranberry using whole-berry cranberry sauce.

Pineapple-cherry dump cake is perfect when served at room temperature, but you can serve it warm or cold as well. A scoop of creamy vanilla ice cream melting on top makes it impossible to resist.

1 (20-ounce) can crushed pineapple in juice (or 1½ cups fresh pineapple chunks)

1 (21-ounce) can cherry pie filling (or 3 pounds fresh sweet cherries, pitted)

1 box yellow cake mix

1 cup shredded coconut

½ cup chopped pecans

1 cup unsalted butter, melted

1. Preheat the oven to 350°F and grease a 13-by-9-inch baking pan.
2. Pour the pineapple into the pan, along with the juice.
3. Add spoonfuls of the cherry pie filling on top of the pineapple.
4. Top with the cake mix.
5. Sprinkle the coconut and pecans over the cake mix.
6. Pour the melted butter over everything.
7. Bake until the top is golden-brown, 30 to 40 minutes.

> **TIP:** Replace the butter with melted organic coconut oil for a dump cake that is low in saturated fat. Coconut oil will give the topping more coconut flavor, which really enhances the tropical feel of this dessert.

CREAM CHEESE

DUMP CAKE

Yield: 12 servings Prep Time: 10 minutes Bake Time: 40–45 minutes

If you like cheesecake, this cream cheese dump cake is going to be very popular around your house! Cherry pie filling is strewn with pieces of cream cheese for that sweet but tangy cheesecake flavor in every bite. You can use yellow cake mix if you prefer, but French vanilla cake mix adds a depth of vanilla that brings out the cheese-cake flavor in this recipe.

Don't use fresh, canned, or frozen cherries in this recipe. You'll need the thicker pie filling to ensure that the cream cheese doesn't completely disappear. Peach pie filling is a good alternative to the cherry pie filling if you want a change of pace.

This is quite rich for a dump cake, so it is best served without any topping at all.

1 box French vanilla cake mix	8 ounces chilled cream cheese
1 (21-ounce) can cherry pie filling	¼ cup unsalted butter, melted

1. Preheat the oven to 350°F and grease a 13-by-9-inch baking pan.
2. Use 2 tablespoons of the cake mix to dust the bottom of the baking pan.
3. Spread the cherry pie filling in the bottom of the pan.
4. Cut the cream cheese into ½-inch cubes, and scatter them over the pie filling.
5. Top with the remaining cake mix.
6. Pour the melted butter over the cake mix.
7. Bake until light brown and bubbly, 40 to 45 minutes.

PIÑA COLADA
···· DUMP CAKE ····

Yield: 12 servings Prep Time: 5 minutes Bake Time: 25–30 minutes

The piña colada is a delicious cocktail that has become a popular flavor for everything from ice cream to chewing gum. Here it is transformed into an easy dump cake with great pineapple and coconut flavor and just a touch of coconut rum to make it taste sensational. If you prefer not to use rum, you can substitute cream of coconut—not coconut milk, but rather the sweetened coconut milk product that is used as a mixer for homemade piña coladas. You can find it in the same aisle as the cocktail mixers, though some stores keep it near the juice or baking supplies.

Although this cake will be delicious any way you serve it, it is especially good served with whipped cream and a maraschino cherry on top.

2 (20-ounce) cans crushed pineapple in juice

1 box coconut cake mix

½ cup unsalted butter, melted

⅓ cup coconut rum

1. Preheat the oven to 375°F and grease a 13-by-9-inch baking pan.

2. Pour the pineapple into the pan, along with the juice, and spread evenly.

3. Top with the cake mix.

4. Whisk the melted butter and rum together, and pour over the cake mix.

5. Bake until light brown and bubbly, 25 to 30 minutes.

TIP: Make this cake special for a barbecue or pool party by garnishing each serving with a miniature cocktail umbrella.

AMBROSIA

······ DUMP CAKE ······

Yield: 12 servings Prep Time: 5 minutes Bake Time: 45–50 minutes

The flavors of this dump cake are taken from a very popular Southern dessert called ambrosia that originated in the Victorian era. It is one of those desserts that every Southern woman creates just a little bit differently. The common denominators, however, are fruit, coconut, and nuts.

Orange cake mix is the one ingredient that gives this dump cake its unique flavor. If you can't find orange cake mix, it is fine to use a white or yellow cake instead. Fruit cocktail is elevated from its humble status and given star quality in this dessert. All of the different fruit flavors mingle together to create a totally new taste that is enhanced by the orange cake mix.

Serve this dump cake with a dollop of lightly sweetened whipped cream.

1 (29-ounce) can fruit cocktail in juice

1 (11-ounce) can mandarin oranges, drained

1 box orange cake mix

½ cup shredded coconut

1 cup chopped pecans

½ cup unsalted butter, melted

1. Preheat the oven to 350°F and grease a 13-by-9-inch baking pan.
2. Pour the fruit cocktail in the bottom of the pan, along with the juice, and spread evenly.
3. Add the mandarin oranges.
4. Top with the cake mix.
5. Sprinkle with the coconut and chopped pecans.
6. Pour the melted butter over the top.
7. Bake until light brown and bubbly, 45 to 50 minutes.

> **TIP:** Many recipes for ambrosia include mini marshmallows. You can stir 1 cup mini marshmallows into the fruit if you like.

KEY LIME

·················· · **DUMP CAKE** · ··················

Yield: 12 servings Prep Time: 10 minutes Bake Time: 45–50 minutes

Key limes are tiny limes that grow in the Florida Keys. They have a very distinct tangy flavor that is hard to miss. You'll get all of that tangy flavor and more in this easy-to-assemble, tropical dessert that is reminiscent of Key lime pie.

The lime cake mix in this recipe enriches the lime flavor of the pie filling, while the graham cracker crumbs give it a little crunch and a hint of sweetness. If you can't find lime cake mix, you can use yellow or white cake mix instead. Lemon pie filling works well in place of the Key lime pie filling if it's not available in your area. The crushed pineapple is included for its texture as much as its flavor.

2 (11-ounce) cans crushed pineapple
   in juice

2 (22-ounce) cans Key lime pie filling

1 box lime cake mix

1 cup graham cracker crumbs

1 cup unsalted butter, melted

1. Preheat the oven to 375°F and grease a 13-by-9-inch baking pan.

2. In a mixing bowl, combine the pineapple and its juice with the lime pie filling and stir well. Spread the mixture in the bottom of the pan.

3. Top with the cake mix.

4. Sprinkle the graham cracker crumbs evenly over the top.

5. Pour the melted butter over everything.

6. Bake until light brown and bubbly, 45 to 50 minutes.

PINEAPPLE UPSIDE-DOWN

· DUMP CAKE ·

Yield: 12 servings Prep Time: 10 minutes Bake Time: 40–45 minutes

The sweet pineapple cake topping gives this cake an added burst of pineapple flavor, and the buttery brown sugar syrup on the bottom will have you licking the pan.

Using pineapple chunks gives the filling a little more texture and pronounced pineapple flavor than crushed pineapple would. The goal is to have an intense flavor of pineapple with random bites of sweet cherries throughout. The pecans can be added to the top of the cake rather than the bottom if you prefer them to stay crunchy.

Serve this cake with a spoonful of lightly sweetened whipped cream on top.

1 cup unsalted butter, divided

2 cups chopped pecans

⅔ cup packed brown sugar

2 (20-ounce) cans pineapple chunks in juice

1 (21-ounce) can cherry pie filling

1 box pineapple cake mix

1. Preheat the oven to 375°F and grease a 13-by-9-inch baking pan.

2. Cut ½ cup of the butter into small pieces, and scatter them over the bottom of the pan.

3. Scatter the pecans over the butter.

4. Cover with an even layer of brown sugar.

5. Pour the pineapple into the pan, along with the juice.

6. Spoon the cherry pie filling over the pineapple.

7. Top with the cake mix.

8. Melt the remaining ½ cup butter, and pour it over everything.

9. Bake until light brown and bubbly, 40 to 45 minutes.

> **TIP:** If you are making homemade whipped cream and want to stabilize it so it won't liquefy in a couple of hours, add a teaspoon or so of pure vanilla extract or white chocolate instant pudding mix when you beat the whipping cream.

TEXAS

·········· DUMP CAKE ··········

*Yield: 12 servings Prep Time: 10 minutes, plus 15 minutes resting time
Bake Time: 50 minutes*

It is a little known fact that Texans are as proud of their peaches as Georgia is of theirs. Several counties produce sweet, juicy peaches that keep Texas bakers making fresh desserts like this one all summer long. Ripe peaches and crunchy pecans are mixed with brown sugar and cinnamon and then covered with butter pecan cake mix. The aroma that wafts from your oven will have your neighbors knocking at your door.

The bourbon in this recipe gives the cake a little kick of unexpected flavor. If you prefer to leave it out, however, you can do so with no other changes to the recipe. Serve Texas dump cake warm with a big scoop of vanilla ice cream.

5 pounds fresh peaches (or two 21-ounce cans peach pie filling)

⅓ cup packed brown sugar

1 teaspoon ground cinnamon

1½ cups chopped pecans

1 box butter pecan cake mix

½ cup unsalted butter, melted

2 tablespoons bourbon

1. Preheat the oven to 350°F and grease a 13-by-9-inch baking pan.

2. Peel, pit, and slice the peaches. Place the peach slices in a bowl.

3. Mix the brown sugar and cinnamon in a small bowl, and then spoon it over the peaches. Stir to coat, and set aside for 15 minutes so the peaches release their juice.

4. Pour the peaches into the pan and spread evenly.

5. Scatter the pecans on top.

6. Top with the cake mix.

7. Whisk the melted butter and bourbon together, and pour over the cake mix.

8. Bake until the top is golden brown, about 50 minutes.

BANANA SPLIT

Yield: 12 servings Prep Time: 10 minutes Bake Time: 45 minutes

Banana splits are as much an American icon as apple pie. Ice cream is layered over ripe bananas and then topped with strawberries, pineapple, chocolate, and nuts. This dump cake has all of those flavors, just in a different order.

This cake has a crispy topping that covers the layers of fruit, chocolate, and nuts. Serve it warm with a scoop of vanilla ice cream and maybe a little hot fudge sauce drizzled over the top. Don't be afraid to substitute chocolate or strawberry ice cream for the vanilla. This is one of those desserts that becomes a family favorite very quickly. It is so easy to make and perfect for potlucks and other large gatherings. You'd better keep this recipe close at hand—you're going to get a lot of requests for it!

2 cups fresh strawberries, thickly sliced

2 tablespoons sugar

1 (20-ounce) can crushed pineapple in juice

6 ripe bananas, thickly sliced

½ cup chopped pecans

½ cup bittersweet chocolate chips

1 box yellow cake mix

1 cup unsalted butter, melted

1. Preheat the oven to 350°F and grease a 13-by-9-inch baking pan.

2. Toss the strawberries with the sugar and set aside.

3. Pour the pineapple into the pan, along with the juice, and spread evenly.

4. Scatter the banana slices over the pineapple.

5. Add the strawberries over the bananas.

6. Sprinkle the pecans and chocolate chips over the berries.

7. Top with the cake mix.

8. Pour the melted butter over the cake mix.

9. Bake until golden-brown, about 45 minutes.

STRAWBERRY-RHUBARB
DUMP CAKE

Yield: 12 servings Prep Time: 10 minutes Bake Time: 45 minutes

Strawberries and rhubarb go together so well because the sweetness of the strawberries balances out the sour tang of the rhubarb. It's one of those things that people either absolutely love or absolutely hate. With this recipe, however, you will almost certainly love it.

Yellow cake mix is whisked with cream soda to bring out its sweetness, but if you prefer a less sweet dessert you can use water instead of the soda. This dump cake comes out more like a cobbler than a crisp, with a cake-like top. If you'd prefer the crumbly topping, leave out the soda and sprinkle the dry cake mix over the fruit, and then drizzle the butter evenly over the top.

Serve this cake warm with a scoop of vanilla ice cream.

1 pound fresh rhubarb,
    cut into bite-sized pieces

1 pound fresh strawberries, quartered

½ cup sugar

1 (3-ounce) package strawberry gelatin

1 box yellow cake mix

1 cup cream soda

½ cup unsalted butter, melted

1. Preheat the oven to 350°F and grease a 13-by-9-inch baking pan.
2. Scatter the rhubarb in the bottom of the pan.
3. Add the strawberries over the rhubarb.
4. Sprinkle the sugar and the gelatin powder over the fruit.
5. In a bowl, whisk together the cake mix, cream soda, and melted butter until well blended. Pour evenly over the fruit.
6. Bake until light brown and bubbly, about 45 minutes.

PIG PICKIN'
DUMP CAKE

Yield: 12 servings Prep Time: 20 minutes Bake Time: 25–30 minutes

This Southern specialty got its name because it was very common at pig roasts and barbecues. Guests "picked" the tender meat off the cooked pig, which is how a Southern barbecue came to be known as a "pig pickin'."

The batter is full of Mandarin oranges and pecans, baked to moist perfection and topped with a delicious frosting made from whipped topping mixed with crushed pineapple and instant pudding. This dump cake is a bit more complicated than some of the others, but the result is well worth it.

FOR THE CAKE

1 box yellow cake mix

½ cup unsalted butter, melted

1 (14-ounce) can Mandarin oranges

4 large eggs, beaten

1 cup chopped pecans

1 teaspoon pure vanilla extract

FOR THE TOPPING

1 (20-ounce) can crushed pineapple in juice

1 (16-ounce) container whipped topping

1 (4-ounce) package instant vanilla pudding mix

TO PREPARE THE CAKE

1. Preheat the oven to 350°F. Grease a 13-by-9-inch baking pan and dust the bottom with flour.

2. In a mixing bowl, combine the cake mix, melted butter, Mandarin oranges with their juice, eggs, pecans, and vanilla. Whisk until smooth. Pour the batter into the baking pan.

3. Bake until golden-brown and set, 25 to 30 minutes.

4. Let cool completely before frosting.

TO PREPARE THE TOPPING

1. In a mixing bowl, beat together the pineapple and juice, whipped topping, and instant pudding mix until smooth.

2. Cover and chill for 1 hour, and then spread over the cooled cake.

3

Big Berries

SUMMERTIME, BERRIES, AND DUMP cakes are a great combination. Ripe berries fill farmers' market stands and grocery store tables, making them the perfect ingredient for summer desserts. Dump cakes are delicious and very fast to make in the morning, which leaves you plenty of time to catch up on your summer reading in the hammock or by the pool. Of course, frozen or canned fruit can be used instead of fresh fruit or pie filling in case you find yourself wanting a blast of summer on a dreary November day.

Choose berries that are clean and bright. Look them over carefully for mold and bruises. Whenever possible, use fresh berries the day you buy them, when their flavor is the freshest. Always remove raspberries and blackberries from their containers and store them on a plate covered with plastic wrap in the refrigerator. These types of berries are very delicate, and the weight of other berries in the container can cause those at the bottom to bruise.

The dump cake recipes in this chapter are designed to make the most of those fresh, tasty berries that you see so much of during the summer. Red Velvet Raspberry Dump Cake has a gorgeous red color and just a touch of chocolate flavor. Or maybe you'd prefer a Blackberry-Merlot or Lemon-Blueberry Dump Cake—whatever kind of berries you like best, you'll find them right here.

BLUEBERRY

······················· DUMP CAKE ·······················

Yield: 12 servings Prep Time: 5 minutes Bake Time: 40 minutes

Choose large, plump blueberries with a white bloom to ensure loads of that sweet blueberry flavor. You may store them carefully in their package in the refrigerator for a day or so, but plan to use them quickly—blueberries will go bad after a few days. If you'd rather use another type of fruit, you can substitute raspberries or strawberries for the blueberries entirely or replace 1 cup of blueberries with another berry to create a blend.

Blueberry dump cake makes the most of bright, sweet berries in the easiest way possible. Serve this cake with a scoop of vanilla ice cream or a dollop of whipped cream sprinkled with a little finely grated lemon zest. Garnish with a fresh mint leaf for color.

4 cups fresh or frozen blueberries (or two 21-ounce cans blueberry pie filling)

½ cup sugar (omit if using pie filling)

1 box white cake mix

¾ cup unsalted butter, melted

1. Preheat the oven to 350°F and grease a 13-by-9-inch baking pan.

2. Spread the blueberries in the bottom of the pan. Add the sugar and mix gently.

3. Top with the cake mix.

4. Pour the melted butter over the cake mix.

5. Bake until cooked through, about 40 minutes.

> TIP: Blueberries are delicious on their own, but try adding finely grated lemon zest for a fresh new taste. Lemon zest enhances the flavor of this recipe and makes the blueberries taste even better.

RASPBERRY

DUMP CAKE

Yield: 12 servings Prep Time: 5 minutes Bake Time: 35–40 minutes

Raspberries and almonds are a classic European pastry combination, and they are just as delicious in this dump cake as they are in a flaky coffee cake.

For a beautiful, elegant, and incredibly easy dessert, serve this cake on a chocolate-drizzled plate with a spoonful of whipped cream on top. To decorate a plate with chocolate drizzle, just take a spoonful of chocolate syrup and make a line across the plate. Make a second line parallel to the first, and repeat the process until the plate is striped with chocolate. Carefully place a scoop of dump cake in the center of the plate and add the whipped cream. You can even grate some chocolate over the whipped cream if you want a little extra flair. Who would be able to say no to that?

6 cups fresh or frozen raspberries
(or two 21-ounce cans raspberry
pie filling)

½ cup sugar (omit if using pie filling)

1 box yellow cake mix

½ cup unsalted butter, melted

1 teaspoon pure almond extract

½ cup sliced almonds

1. Preheat the oven to 350°F and grease a 13-by-9-inch baking pan.

2. Spread the raspberries in the bottom of the pan. Add the sugar and mix gently.

3. Top with the cake mix.

4. Whisk the melted butter and almond extract together, and pour over the cake mix.

5. Sprinkle the almonds over the top.

6. Bake until set, 35 to 40 minutes.

RED VELVET RASPBERRY

· DUMP CAKE ·

Yield: 12 servings Prep Time: 5 minutes Bake Time: 35–40 minutes

Red velvet cake has a delicate chocolate flavor and, when it is done right, a unique crimson color. This cake is beautiful when combined with ripe red raspberries and a generous puff of white whipped cream on top.

This recipe makes an extra-special Valentine's Day dessert, but it is so simple that you can throw it together after work and have it ready for a romantic dinner. The faint cocoa flavor in this recipe combines with the lush raspberries to make this cake something that won't easily be forgotten.

6 cups fresh or frozen raspberries
(or two 21-ounce cans raspberry
pie filling)

½ cup sugar (omit if using pie filling)

1 box red velvet cake mix

½ cup unsalted butter, melted

1. Preheat the oven to 350°F and grease a 13-by-9-inch baking pan.

2. Spread the raspberries in the bottom of the pan. Add the sugar and mix gently.

3. Top with the cake mix.

4. Pour the melted butter over the cake mix.

5. Bake until set, 35 to 40 minutes.

TIP: Cream cheese frosting makes for an unusual but delicious topping for this dump cake. Make this frosting by whipping 8 ounces softened cream cheese with ¼ cup heavy whipping cream and a tablespoon or so of sugar until the mixture has the texture of thick whipped cream.

BLACKBERRY-MERLOT

DUMP CAKE

Yield: 12 servings Prep Time: 5 minutes Bake Time: 35–40 minutes

Just because dump cake is an easy-to-prepare, home-style comfort food, that doesn't mean you can't dress it up a little when the occasion calls for it. This dump cake has a sophisticated flavor that is just as much at home on a white linen–covered banquet table as it is on a picnic blanket. The wine adds complexity to the dessert while enhancing the ripe blackberry flavor. If you don't wish to use wine you may substitute grape juice, or omit the extra liquid completely.

Serve this dump cake while it is slightly warm, with a scoop of vanilla bean ice cream on top. This flavorful recipe doesn't need a lot of garnish—the deep purple hue of the fruit offset by the vanilla ice cream is gorgeous just as it is.

5 cups fresh or frozen blackberries
  (or two 21-ounce cans blackberry
  pie filling)

½ cup sugar (omit if using pie filling)

½ cup Merlot

1 box white cake mix

½ cup unsalted butter, melted

1. Preheat the oven to 350°F and grease a 13-by-9-inch baking pan.

2. Spread the blackberries in the bottom of the pan. Add the sugar and Merlot, and mix gently.

3. Top with the cake mix.

4. Pour the melted butter over the cake mix.

5. Bake until set, 35 to 40 minutes.

VERY BERRY

······················· DUMP CAKE ·······················

Yield: 12 servings Prep Time: 5 minutes Bake Time: 30–35 minutes

Here's a dump cake that is bursting with all kinds of fresh summer berries. Sweet blueberries, tangy raspberries, and juicy strawberries work together to make this dessert absolutely delicious. If you have other berries on hand—like loganberries, blackberries, or even elderberries—you can swap them in for some of the fruit called for in the recipe or even replace them entirely with what you have on hand.

Unfortunately, pie fillings don't work well in this recipe because they are so thick that the fruit doesn't mix properly and the flavor gets muddied. Use fresh or frozen fruit for the best results. Keep in mind that you may not need the full amount of sugar, depending on which type of berries you use. Add a few tablespoons at a time and taste until you have it just right.

1½ cups fresh or frozen blueberries

1½ cups fresh or frozen raspberries

1 cup fresh or frozen strawberries, sliced

½ cup sugar

1 box yellow cake mix

½ cup unsalted butter, melted

1. Preheat the oven to 350°F and grease a 13-by-9-inch baking pan.

2. Spread the berries in the bottom of the pan. Add the sugar and mix gently.

3. Top with the cake mix.

4. Pour the melted butter over the cake mix.

5. Bake until set, 30 to 35 minutes.

> **TIP:** Frozen berries work very well when fresh berries aren't in season or when your selection is limited. You'll need about 3 pounds frozen berries for this recipe.

LEMON-BLUEBERRY

DUMP CAKE

Yield: 12 servings Prep Time: 5 minutes Bake Time: 30–35 minutes

The flavors of lemon and blueberry are fantastic together because the sweetness of the blueberries balances the acidity of the lemon and creates a whole new flavor profile. This dump cake uses that synergy to its best advantage with both Meyer lemon in the filling and lemon-flavored cake mix on top. This dessert has big flavor that's bound to please both the blueberry and lemon fans in your circle of friends and family.

If you do not have lemon cake mix, yellow cake mix can be substituted in this recipe. Pistachio nuts are a delicious addition to the cake, giving it a unique, almost tropical flavor. Just sprinkle about ½ cup chopped toasted pistachios over the topping before baking.

2 (21-ounce) cans blueberry pie filling (or 5 cups fresh or frozen blueberries)

Juice and zest of 1 large Meyer lemon

1 box lemon cake mix

½ cup unsalted butter, melted

1. Preheat the oven to 350°F and grease a 13-by-9-inch baking pan.

2. Spread the blueberry pie filling in the bottom of the pan. Add the lemon juice and zest, and stir gently.

3. Top with the cake mix.

4. Pour the melted butter over the cake mix.

5. Bake until set, 30 to 35 minutes.

TIP: Meyer lemons are a cross between a lemon and a Mandarin orange, so they have the tartness of lemons blended with the subtle sweetness of orange. If you can't find Meyer lemons, you can substitute a regular lemon in this recipe.

FOURTH OF JULY

· DUMP CAKE ·

Yield: 12 servings Prep Time: 5 minutes Bake Time: 45 minutes

When you are feeling particularly patriotic, this cherry and blueberry dump cake recipe is the one you'll be pulling out of your favorite recipe file. Crimson cherry pie filling is topped with sweet, ripe blueberries to create a colorful layered cake—if you mix the ingredients, the colors will be less distinct. This cake is made with white cake mix and drizzled with melted butter so that the topping is sweet, buttery, and a little crumbly.

Add a scoop of vanilla ice cream and some red, white, and blue sprinkles for a festive Fourth of July dessert that is quick and easy to prepare. Since this recipe comes together in minutes and bakes while you are putting the finishing touches on the rest of your meal, you'll be free to enjoy the party with everyone else.

2 (21-ounce) cans cherry pie filling

1½ cups fresh or frozen blueberries

1 box white cake mix

1 cup unsalted butter, melted

1. Preheat the oven to 325°F and grease a 13-by-9-inch baking pan.

2. Spread the cherry pie filling in the bottom of the pan.

3. Scatter the blueberries over the cherry pie filling.

4. Top with the cake mix.

5. Pour the melted butter over the cake mix.

6. Bake until set, about 45 minutes. Cool the cake slightly before serving.

LEMON-LIME SODA
DUMP CAKE

Yield: 12 servings *Prep Time:* 5 minutes, plus 5 minutes resting time
Bake Time: 45–50 minutes

A fizzy can of lemon-lime soda gives this cake a different flavor and texture than most of the other dump cakes in this book. Since this recipe doesn't require any butter, it is lower in fat and calories, too! You can lower the calories even more by using sugar-free cake mix and sugar-free soda—this will also make the cake diabetic-friendly.

The one thing you'll need to be careful about with this recipe is the soda—make sure it completely covers the cake mix so there are no dry spots after the mixture sits for 5 minutes. If there are dry spots, simply pour a little more soda over the dry areas and let it soak in. Serve this cake with a dollop of whipped cream or a big scoop of vanilla ice cream.

2 pounds fresh or frozen mixed berries   1 (12-ounce) can lemon-lime soda

1 box white cake mix

1. Preheat the oven to 350°F and grease a 13-by-9-inch baking pan.

2. Spread the berries in the bottom of the pan.

3. Top with the cake mix.

4. Carefully pour the soda over the cake mix, making sure to cover it completely. Let stand for 5 minutes.

5. Bake until set, 45 to 50 minutes. Allow the cake to cool to room temperature before serving.

> **TIP:** This recipe is also delicious when you use sliced apples or peaches in place of the berries. You might also try substituting a box of spice cake mix and ginger ale for the white cake and lemon-lime soda to create a delicious autumn variation of this easy recipe.

BLUEBERRY CRUNCH

··· DUMP CAKE ·······································

Yield: 12 *servings* **Prep Time:** *5 minutes* **Bake Time:** *45–55 minutes*

Sweet blueberries with a delicate sugar glaze are layered on top of juicy pineapple and covered with yellow cake mix and pecans. The whole thing is then drizzled with melted butter. Once baked, this dump cake is sweet, crumbly, and just a little tangy from the pineapple.

Don't use canned pie filling with this recipe; fresh blueberries are best, but frozen will work if you have no other option. What makes this recipe unique is that the blueberries are coated with butter and sugar to form a glaze as they bake. The cake mix itself, along with the nuts, add another layer of crunch to this delicious dessert. Feel free to use walnuts in place of the pecans called for in this recipe if you prefer them.

Lightly sweetened whipped cream or whipped topping is a sweet way to garnish the finished cake.

··

1 pound fresh or frozen blueberries

½ cup plus 1 tablespoon unsalted butter, melted, divided

¾ cup sugar

1 (20-ounce) can crushed pineapple in juice

1 cup chopped pecans

··

1. Preheat the oven to 350°F and grease a 13-by-9-inch baking pan.

2. Combine the blueberries and 1 tablespoon of the melted butter in a mixing bowl. Sprinkle with the sugar and stir gently to coat the blueberries.

3. Pour the pineapple into the pan, along with the juice, and spread evenly.

4. Cover the pineapple with the blueberries.

5. Top with the cake mix.

6. Pour the remaining ½ cup melted butter over the cake mix.

7. Scatter the pecans over everything.

8. Bake until the top is browned, 45 to 55 minutes.

RASPBERRY-PEACH MELBA
DUMP CAKE

Yield: 12 servings Prep Time: 5 minutes Bake Time: 35–40 minutes

Peach Melba is an enticing dessert that consists of peaches and raspberries served over vanilla ice cream. This dish was created by Auguste Escoffier in the early 1880s to honor a singer by the name of Nellie Melba. Over the years the dish became famous and has been used as inspiration for a number of tasty desserts. There aren't many desserts created by famous French chefs that are as easy to prepare as this dump cake!

Inspired by Escoffier's dessert, this dump cake is a mouthwatering combination of sweet peaches, plump raspberries, and a delicious vanilla topping. Add a scoop of vanilla ice cream to the top to complete the peach Melba theme. Pears, apricots, and mango can be easily substituted for the peaches in this recipe, if you prefer.

1 (21-ounce) can peach pie filling (or 2 pounds fresh peaches, peeled, pitted, and sliced)

3 cups fresh or frozen raspberries

1 box French vanilla cake mix

1 teaspoon pure vanilla extract

½ cup unsalted butter, melted

1. Preheat the oven to 350°F and grease a 13-by-9-inch baking pan.
2. Spread the peach pie filling in the bottom of the pan.
3. Add the raspberries on top of the peach pie filling but do not stir.
4. Top with the cake mix.
5. Whisk the vanilla into the melted butter, and pour it over the cake mix.
6. Bake until set, 35 to 40 minutes.

TIP: To give this dessert an extra-special flourish, drizzle it with raspberry syrup. To make the syrup, simply heat raspberry jam until it becomes a liquid and drizzle it over the top of the cake. To finish the presentation, sprinkle with chopped toasted almonds.

STRABWERRY MARGARITA
DUMP CAKE

Yield: 12 servings Prep Time: 15 minutes Bake Time: 40–45 minutes

A frozen margarita is to many adults what an ice pop is to children in the summertime—sweet, tangy, ice cold, and totally refreshing! There is no alcohol in this recipe, but there is plenty of flavor. Top this cake off with a big scoop of strawberry ice cream to serve.

This dump cake has a couple of extra steps, so it may take a little longer to assemble than other recipes, but the finished product is well worth it. Be sure to use margarita mix instead of water when following the instructions to prepare the boxed cake mix.

5 cups fresh strawberries, quartered

1 (3-ounce) package strawberry gelatin

1¼ cups non-alcoholic strawberry margarita mix, divided

1 box strawberry cake mix

Ingredients called for on cake mix box

1. Preheat the oven to 350°F and grease a 13-by-9-inch baking pan.

2. Combine the strawberries, gelatin, and ¼ cup of the strawberry margarita mix in a large mixing bowl and stir well. Spread the strawberry mixture in the bottom of the pan.

3. Follow the preparation instructions on the box of cake mix, but substitute the remaining 1 cup strawberry margarita mix for the water called for in the recipe. Spoon the batter over the fruit.

4. Bake until a toothpick inserted in the center of the cake comes out clean, 40 to 45 minutes. Let the cake cool for 20 minutes before serving.

BLUEBERRY-CREAM CHEESE
DUMP CAKE

Yield: 12 servings Prep Time: 10 minutes Bake Time: 40–45 minutes

Packed with sweet blueberries and chunks of rich cream cheese, this dump cake will remind you of a blueberry cheesecake with every bite you take. There is a parade of flavor in every spoonful, starting with the blueberry and ending with the faint flavor of cream cheese.

You can swap in any of your favorite fruit pie fillings for the blueberries in this recipe—strawberry or peach pie fillings are particularly good substitutions. You'll need the cream cheese to rest on top of the fruit, so this recipe is best made with pie filling rather than fresh, frozen, or canned fruit.

1 (21-ounce) can blueberry pie filling

8 ounces chilled cream cheese

1 box yellow cake mix

¼ cup unsalted butter

1. Preheat the oven to 350°F and grease a 13-by-9-inch baking pan.

2. Spread the blueberry pie filling in the bottom of the pan.

3. Cut the cream cheese into small cubes, and scatter them over the pie filling.

4. Top with the cake mix.

5. Slice the butter thinly and scatter the slices over the cake mix.

6. Bake until golden, 40 to 45 minutes. Let the cake cool for 15 minutes before serving.

> **TIP:** To add a festive look to any dump cake, simply use a cake mix that contains sprinkles. You can also add your own sprinkles to any mix.

4

Chocolate Delights

THERE ARE VERY FEW people who don't love chocolate. It has been a popular ingredient since the ancient Olmec people first tasted cacao beans in 1800 B.C.

Chocolate can be smooth and mild, deep and seductive, or a sweet combination of the two. It combines well with most kinds of fruit and there is just something about a chocolate dessert that makes any day a little more special. If you've been depending on brownies and instant chocolate pudding for your quick chocolate fix, you'll be happy to have this list of 12 luscious chocolate desserts that you can put together in a flash. There is also virtually no cleanup!

In this chapter designed for chocolate lovers you'll find dump cake recipes that are as simple as Fudgy Chocolate Dump Cake as well as recipes that skillfully combine chocolate and other ingredients to mimic trendy flavor combinations, like Salted Caramel–Chocolate Dump Cake. There are also comfort food favorites like S'mores and German Chocolate. In other words, if you can't get enough chocolate, then you've found the right chapter.

FUDGY CHOCOLATE

·· DUMP CAKE ··································

Yield: 12 *servings* *Prep Time:* 5 *minutes* *Bake Time:* 30 *minutes*

This deep, dark, fudgy chocolate cake takes almost no time at all to prepare. You simply open a few boxes, tear open a couple of bags, and dump some milk into a measuring cup. It takes longer to read this recipe than it does to put it together!

You will notice that two kinds of chocolate chips are called for in the recipe because, together, they create a deeper and more complex chocolate flavor than if you use just one kind. If you only have one type of chocolate chips on hand, however, your cake will not be greatly affected.

1 cup bittersweet chocolate chips

½ cup semisweet chocolate chips

1 box chocolate cake mix

1 (3-ounce) package chocolate fudge pudding mix

1½ cups milk

1. Preheat the oven to 350°F and grease a 13-by-9-inch baking pan.

2. Combine the bittersweet and semisweet chocolate chips in a small bowl.

3. In a large mixing bowl, combine the cake mix, pudding mix, milk, and half of the chocolate chips and stir until well combined. Spread the mixture in the baking pan.

4. Sprinkle with the remaining chocolate chips.

5. Bake until the cake pulls away from the sides of the pan, about 30 minutes.

> **TIP:** Serve this cake warm with a scoop of chocolate ice cream and hot fudge sauce for the ultimate chocolate-loaded dessert. It's guaranteed to quell even the strongest chocolate craving.

BLACK FOREST

DUMP CAKE

Yield: 12 servings Prep Time: 10 minutes Bake Time: 1 hour

Black Forest cake originated in Germany and is now the best known German cake in the world. In Europe, Black Forest cake is often made with cherry brandy or kirsch, but in the United States it is typically alcohol-free.

Traditional Black Forest cake consists of layers of chocolate and cherries with a whipped cream frosting and takes a long time to make. This Black Forest dump cake, however, has all of the chocolate and cherry flavor with none of the work. The cherry pie filling is a sweet contrast to the chocolate cake, and the hot fudge just adds to the chocolate overload contained within this dessert. Serve this cake warm with a spoonful of whipped cream, grated chocolate, and a maraschino cherry on top.

2 (21-ounce) cans cherry pie filling (or 4½ pounds fresh sweet cherries, pitted)

1 box chocolate cake mix

¾ cup unsalted butter, melted

1 cup hot fudge sauce

1. Preheat the oven to 350°F and grease a 13-by-9-inch baking pan.

2. Spread the cherry pie filling in the bottom of the pan.

3. Top with the cake mix.

4. Pour the melted butter over the cake mix.

5. Warm the hot fudge in a microwave-safe bowl in the microwave in 10-second intervals until it liquefies. Pour the melted hot fudge over top of the cake.

6. Bake until set, about 1 hour.

RASPBERRY-CHOCOLATE TRUFFLE
DUMP CAKE

Yield: 12 *servings* *Prep Time:* 5 *minutes* *Bake Time:* 35–40 *minutes*

Red raspberries and dark chocolate are an elegant combination, no matter what form they take. In this easy recipe the raspberry-chocolate combination, along with a cup of cola, creates a moist, rich chocolate dessert with the unmistakable flavor of red raspberry. The cola enhances the chocolate flavor, but if you are really a fan of raspberry there is no reason why you can't use raspberry soda instead.

It is important to use dark chocolate cake mix for this recipe—don't choose milk chocolate, because it won't hold up to the raspberry flavor. Chocolate fudge, dark chocolate, or devil's food cake mixes are the best options. If you feel that there are not enough raspberries in this recipe, you can add 1 cup fresh or frozen berries to the canned raspberries.

1 (15-ounce) can red raspberries in syrup

1 box dark chocolate cake mix

1 cup dark chocolate chips

1 cup cola

1. Preheat the oven to 350°F and grease a 13-by-9-inch baking pan.

2. Pour the raspberries into the pan, along with the syrup, and spread evenly.

3. In a large bowl, quickly mix the cake mix, chocolate chips, and cola. Spoon the mixture over the raspberries.

4. Bake until a toothpick inserted in the center comes out clean, 35 to 40 minutes. Cool for at least 15 minutes before serving.

TIP: Add a tablespoon or two of Chambord raspberry liqueur to enhance the raspberry flavor of this recipe. Just drizzle the liqueur over the berries before adding the cake batter.

CHOCOLATE CHIP
DUMP CAKE

Yield: 12 servings Prep Time: 5 minutes Bake Time: 30 minutes

Chocolate chip cookies are one of the top treats on everyone's list. When making homemade chocolate chip cookies, you may find it almost impossible to avoid the temptation to eat at least a few bites of the dough. In some ways, chocolate chip cookie dough is becoming more popular as a dessert flavor than chocolate chip cookies are themselves!

This recipe is like a huge, warm, gooey chocolate chip cookie. It has the old-fashioned flavor of homemade chocolate chip cookies along with lots of meltingly warm chocolate chips. Best of all, it will take you mere seconds to put together. Serve this cake warm with a scoop of vanilla ice cream and a drizzle of hot fudge for a family dessert that you'll be asked to make again and again.

1 cup bittersweet chocolate chips

1 cup semisweet chocolate chips

1 box yellow cake mix

1 (3-ounce) package butterscotch pudding mix

1½ cups milk

1. Preheat the oven to 350°F and grease a 13-by-9-inch baking pan.

2. Combine the bittersweet and semisweet chocolate chips in a small bowl.

3. In a large mixing bowl, combine the cake mix, pudding mix, milk, and half of the chocolate chips and stir well. Spread the mixture in the baking pan.

4. Sprinkle with the remaining chocolate chips.

5. Bake until the cake pulls away from the sides of the pan, about 30 minutes. Cool for 10 minutes before serving.

WHITE CHOCOLATE-RASPBERRY
DUMP CAKE

Yield: 12 servings Prep Time: 5 minutes Bake Time: 35–40 minutes

White chocolate isn't actually made from cocoa beans, but it does contain cocoa butter. It has a smooth, creamy texture and very sweet flavor, which, in this recipe, balances the flavor of tart fruit.

Don't be fooled by the minimal ingredient list for this recipe—this dump cake may be simple but it is as rich as they come. White cake mix is combined with white chocolate pudding mix, cream soda, and white chocolate chips to make a rich, moist cake that cooks over tangy red raspberry pie filling. It makes an elegant and unique cobbler-type dessert when served with a dollop of lightly sweetened whipped cream. You can replace the raspberry pie filling with an equal amount of the berry pie filling of your choice.

1 (21-ounce) can raspberry pie filling

1 box white cake mix

1 (3-ounce) package white chocolate or vanilla pudding mix

1 cup cream soda

2 cups white chocolate chips

1. Preheat the oven to 350°F and grease a 13-by-9-inch baking pan.

2. Spread the raspberry pie filling in the bottom of the pan.

3. In a large mixing bowl, combine the cake mix, pudding mix, soda, and white chocolate chips and stir. Spread the mixture over the raspberries in the pan.

4. Bake until a toothpick inserted in the center comes out clean, 35 to 40 minutes. Cool for 10 minutes before serving.

TIP: Though this recipe yields a cobbler-like dessert, you can make it a little more "cakey" by using 2 cups fresh raspberries in place of the pie filling. Fold the fresh berries into the cake batter along with the white chocolate chips, and bake as directed.

DEVIL'S FOOD

· DUMP CAKE ·

Yield: 12 servings Prep Time: 5 minutes Bake Time: 25–30 minutes

Chocolate, chocolate, and more chocolate can be found in every bite of this simple chocolate dump cake. It takes about a minute to get it ready for baking and, when it comes out of the oven, it is light, moist, and . . . well . . . chocolaty.

This recipe also has a long list of possible variations. Instead of chocolate chips, try chopped peanut butter cups, candy bars, or candy-coated chocolates. Root beer is the soda of choice in this recipe, but cola can be substituted if you prefer. Each one of these substitutions changes the flavor and texture of the cake into something a little different.

Serve this cake with a scoop of your favorite ice cream or a dollop of whipped cream for an anytime snack.

1 box moist-style devil's food or chocolate cake mix

1 (12-ounce) can root beer

2 cups bittersweet chocolate chips

1. Preheat the oven to 350°F and grease a 13-by-9-inch baking pan.

2. Combine the cake mix and the root beer in a large bowl, stirring until smooth. Spoon the batter into the baking pan.

3. Top with the chocolate chips.

4. Bake until a toothpick inserted in the center comes out clean, 25 to 30 minutes.

S'MORES

Yield: 12 servings Prep Time: 5 minutes Bake Time: 30 minutes

One of the most memorable desserts of childhood has got to be s'mores. Gooey marshmallows with a charred and crispy outside, squished between two graham crackers along with a square of warm chocolate is a summer dessert that just makes you smile. This dump cake gives you all of that flavor with minimal effort—which should make you smile even more.

This dump cake has a rich, chewy texture, and the chocolate chips add even more chocolate flavor. For the best flavor, you should plan on serving this cake warm so the marshmallows and chocolate on top are still gooey and messy—exactly how s'mores should be. This cake doesn't need ice cream or whipped cream because the toasted marshmallows and graham crackers on the top are really all that you'll want.

1 box chocolate cake mix

1 (3-ounce) package chocolate pudding mix

1½ cups milk

2 cups bittersweet chocolate chips, divided

1½ cups mini marshmallows, divided

1 cup coarsely broken graham crackers

1. Preheat the oven to 350°F and grease a 13-by-9-inch baking pan.

2. In a large mixing bowl, combine the cake mix, pudding mix, milk, 1 cup of the chocolate chips, and ½ cup of the marshmallows and stir. Spread the mixture in the bottom of the baking pan.

3. Sprinkle the batter with the graham crackers and the remaining 1 cup chocolate chips.

4. Bake until set, about 25 minutes.

5. Sprinkle the remaining 1 cup marshmallows on top, and bake until the cake pulls away from the sides of the pan, about 5 minutes more.

> **TIP:** If the marshmallows don't have a chance to turn golden-brown during the last few minutes of baking time, you can use a kitchen torch to toast them to perfection.

SALTED CARAMEL-CHOCOLATE
DUMP CAKE

Yield: 12 servings   Prep Time: 10 minutes   Bake Time: 40–50 minutes

In this dump cake, chewy caramel candies top a rich, moist chocolate cake. The cake is sprinkled with vanilla sea salt and chocolate chips just before baking. When you are using salt in a recipe like this, it is important to remember that you won't need much—a little goes a long way.

You cannot substitute regular salt for the sea salt in this recipe. Traditional table salt crystals are too small, and your delicious dessert will end up tasting like you accidently spilled salt into the batter when you were mixing up the cake. Fleur de sel or a similar sea salt is flaked, not finely ground, so it has a delicate crunch and is made for garnishing and finishing dishes like this dump cake.

1 (3-ounce) package instant chocolate pudding

1½ cups milk

1 box chocolate cake mix

2 cups caramel candies, quartered

Flaked vanilla sea salt

1 cup bittersweet chocolate chips

1. Preheat the oven to 350°F and grease a 13-by-9-inch baking pan.

2. Whisk together the pudding and milk in a large mixing bowl until just combined. Stir in the cake mix. Pour the batter into the baking pan.

3. Scatter the caramels over the batter.

4. Sprinkle lightly with vanilla sea salt.

5. Top with the chocolate chips.

6. Bake until a toothpick inserted in the center comes out clean, 40 to 50 minutes.

> **TIP**: Vanilla sea salt is a flaked salt that has been infused with vanilla bean. The vanilla bean gives it just a hint of vanilla flavor that works well in recipes like this. If you cannot find vanilla sea salt, any other coarsely ground or flaked sea salt will do.

CHOCOLATE-CHERRY COLA

··· DUMP CAKE ·······································

Yield: 12 servings Prep Time: 5 minutes Bake Time: 35–40 minutes

If you love chocolate-covered cherries, then you'll love this cake. Sweet maraschino cherries are covered with a dark chocolate cake batter and baked to perfection. When the cake is removed from the oven, the entire house smells heavenly and you have a moist, chocolaty dessert with almost no cleanup. The cherry cola in this recipe enhances the flavor of the cherries while giving the cake a wonderfully light texture.

If you prefer not to use whole maraschino cherries, you can substitute a 21-ounce can of cherry pie filling or 1 pound frozen cherries. Serve this cake with a scoop of ice cream or whipped cream on top of each piece. If you are using ice cream, you can even add a drizzle of hot fudge.

1 (16-ounce) jar maraschino cherries in juice, stems removed

1 box devil's food cake mix

1 cup cherry cola

1. Preheat the oven to 350°F and grease a 13-by-9-inch baking pan.

2. Pour the cherries and their juice into the pan.

3. Whisk together the cake mix and soda in a large mixing bowl until well combined. Pour the batter over the cherries in the pan.

4. Bake until a toothpick inserted in the center comes out clean, 35 to 40 minutes. Cool the cake for 20 minutes before serving.

GERMAN CHOCOLATE

· DUMP CAKE ·

Yield: 12 servings Prep Time: 10 minutes Bake Time: 40–50 minutes

German chocolate cake is not German at all. It was named for the type of baking chocolate Sam German created for the Hershey's chocolate company in 1852. The cake itself was developed by a home cook in Texas in 1954 and has been a favorite since then. German chocolate cake consists of layers of chocolate cake separated by layers of a caramel-coconut-pecan mixture, which also serves as frosting. This dump cake provides those same flavors but in an easy form.

Tender coconut and crunchy pecans are spread in the bottom of the baking pan, and the cake mix and chocolate chips are stirred in for good measure. Finally, a cream cheese mixture is spread over the top of the entire cake. Using this recipe, gooey, warm chocolate comfort can be yours in less than an hour.

· ·

2 cups shredded unsweetened coconut	1 cup semisweet chocolate chips
2 cups chopped pecans	8 ounces cream cheese, softened
1 box German chocolate cake mix	½ cup unsalted butter, melted
Ingredients called for on cake mix box	3¾ cups confectioners' sugar

· ·

1. Preheat the oven to 350°F and grease a 13-by-9-inch baking pan.

2. Sprinkle the coconut and pecans in the bottom of the pan.

3. Prepare the cake mix as directed and stir in the chocolate chips. Pour the batter evenly over the coconut and pecans.

4. In a mixing bowl, beat the cream cheese, melted butter, and confectioners' sugar until smooth. Spoon the mixture over the batter and gently smooth the surface.

5. Bake until set, 40 to 50 minutes.

TIP: To get more flavor from your coconut and pecans, toast them in a 350°F oven until they turn golden-brown, about 10 minutes. Watch them carefully because they'll burn quickly.

BAILEYS CHOCOLATE

· DUMP CAKE ·

Yield: 12 servings Prep Time: 5 minutes Bake Time: 30 minutes

Baileys Irish Cream liqueur is a combination of Irish whiskey and cream with sweetener and other flavors added. It tastes a bit like chocolate, a bit like coffee, and a whole lot like creamy whiskey goodness. Using this liqueur in a chocolate cake brings all of that flavor into the cake and makes it moist, too.

If you'd like the flavor of Baileys but prefer not to use the alcohol, you can use an Irish cream coffee creamer. In place of the milk and the Baileys called for in this recipe, substitute $1\frac{1}{2}$ cups Irish cream coffee creamer instead. It won't taste exactly the same, but it will still be moist and delicious. Serve this cake with a dollop of whipped cream on top and a steaming cup of coffee on the side.

1 box chocolate fudge cake mix

1 (3-ounce) package chocolate fudge pudding mix

1 cup milk

½ cup Baileys Irish Cream

1 cup bittersweet chocolate chips

1. Preheat the oven to 350°F and grease a 13-by-9-inch baking pan.

2. In a large mixing bowl, combine the cake mix, pudding mix, milk, and Baileys and stir. Spread the mixture in the baking pan.

3. Sprinkle the chocolate chips over the top.

4. Bake until the cake pulls away from the sides of the pan, about 30 minutes.

ROCKY ROAD

DUMP CAKE

Yield: 12 servings Prep Time: 15 minutes Bake Time: 55–60 minutes

Rocky Road got its name during the Depression when the creator, William Dreyer, decided to "give people something to smile about" in the midst of a very difficult time. This flavor traditionally includes chocolate, coconut, marshmallows, and almonds. If you prefer walnuts or pecans, you can substitute them for the almonds in this recipe.

This dump cake doesn't require any additional topping. Just like an upside-down cake, you simply flip it over onto a tray and the chocolate, coconut, and almonds are then on top. The marshmallows melt into the topping so that the sticky sweet flavor is there, but you can't see them. Serve this cake warm with a big scoop of chocolate ice cream. The gooey topping, crunchy nuts, warm cake, and cold ice cream all work together to make this cake one that you won't easily forget.

---

1 box chocolate fudge cake mix

Ingredients called for on cake mix box

1¼ cups brewed coffee

¼ cup unsalted butter

1 cup packed brown sugar

1 cup shredded unsweetened coconut

1 cup chopped almonds

2 cups semisweet chocolate chips

2 cups mini marshmallows

---

1. Preheat the oven to 325°F and grease a 13-by-9-inch baking pan.

2. Prepare the cake mix according to the instructions on the package and set aside.

3. Heat the coffee and butter in a small saucepan over medium-low heat until the butter has melted. Remove from the heat and whisk in the brown sugar.

4. Pour the butter mixture into the baking pan.

5. Add the coconut, almonds, chocolate chips, and marshmallows.

6. Pour the cake batter over the top.

7. Bake until set, 55 to 60 minutes. Cool the cake for 10 minutes.

8. Place a platter or tray over the top of the cake, and flip to dump the cake out onto the tray with the coconut side up.

5

Fall Flavors

BY NOW YOU KNOW that dump cakes come in a variety of textures, flavors, and preparation steps. The desserts in this chapter are those that have a cozy autumn feel. Made with ingredients like maple syrup, pumpkin, and cranberries, these dump cakes are delicious enough to have a starring role on your holiday dessert table but easy enough that you can make them any day of the week.

Apples, pumpkins, cranberries, and pecans are all plentiful in the fall if you want to use fresh ingredients rather than canned. In some cases, as with pumpkin and cranberry, you'll need to cook the ingredients before you can use them in the recipes.

Pie pumpkins, also called sugar pumpkins, are easily prepared by cutting them in half, removing the seeds and membranes, and baking them at 375°F, cut side down, until the flesh is tender. You can then scoop it out and use it in place of canned pumpkin purée in these recipes.

Instead of canned cranberry sauce, you can cook fresh cranberries with 1 cup sugar and 1 cup water, stirring often, until they pop open easily when you put pressure on them with a spoon.

Dump cakes with autumn flavors are perfect for those office holiday parties and church potlucks. Keep the ingredients on hand and you'll be able to create dessert no matter how busy you are.

CARAMEL APPLE
DUMP CAKE

Yield: 12 servings Prep Time: 5 minutes Bake Time: 35–40 minutes

Sweet apple pie filling is mixed with just enough apple cider vinegar to give it a little zip and then drizzled with caramel sauce. Add the dry cake mix, some pecans, and butter and you will have created a dessert that tastes like those huge caramel apples you get at the state fair every year. This cake is delicious when served warm and topped with vanilla ice cream. Add a little caramel drizzle to the top of the ice cream before serving.

If you'll be using fresh apples in this recipe, make sure to bake the cake until the apples are fork-tender. Use Granny Smith, Honey Crisp, or other tangy apples that hold their shape when cooked. Sweeten the apples with sugar to taste before baking.

---

2 (21-ounce) cans apple pie filling
(or 4 pounds fresh apples, peeled, cored, and sliced)

1 teaspoon apple cider vinegar

¼ cup caramel sauce

1 box yellow cake mix

½ cup chopped pecans

1 cup unsalted butter, melted

---

1. Preheat the oven to 350°F and grease a 13-by-9-inch baking pan.

2. Spread the apple pie filling in the bottom of the pan, and stir in the apple cider vinegar.

3. Drizzle the caramel sauce over the apples.

4. Top with the cake mix.

5. Scatter the pecans over the cake mix.

6. Pour the melted butter over everything.

7. Bake until the center of the cake is set, 35 to 40 minutes.

> **TIP:** For an added depth of flavor, you can use a box of spice cake instead of yellow cake mix. The resulting cake may not taste so much like a caramel apple, but it will be spicy and delicious.

SLOW COOKER SPICED APPLE
DUMP CAKE

Yield: 12 servings Prep Time: 5 minutes Cook Time: 4 hours

Slow cookers are simple appliances that make life infinitely easier. Most people don't use their slow cookers as much as they could, simply because they are kept out of sight on a high shelf or on top of the refrigerator where they are easy to forget about. While most people think of slow cookers as good for making delicious roasts and stews, you can also make wonderfully easy desserts like this dump cake.

This cake is more like an apple crisp than a cake—the apples are sweet and tender while the topping is crisp and spicy. If you are using fresh apples rather than apple pie filling, you'll need to give the cake more time to cook.

If you have a slow cooker with a programmable timer, you can set it to start 5 hours before you get home and hold it on warm when it's finished. This way you don't have to worry about the cake becoming overcooked.

2 (21-ounce) cans apple pie filling
(or 4 pounds fresh apples, peeled, cored, and sliced)

1 box spice cake mix

½ cup unsalted butter, melted

½ cup chopped pecans

1. Spray the crockery insert of a 4-quart slow cooker with cooking spray.

2. Spread the apple pie filling in the bottom of the slow cooker.

3. In a mixing bowl, stir together the cake mix, melted butter, and pecans until they are crumbly. Sprinkle the mixture over the apples.

4. Cover and cook on low for 4 hours or on high for 2 hours.

> **TIP:** Nuts are tastier if you take a little time to toast them in the oven. To do so, spread them in a single layer on a baking sheet, and bake at 350°F until golden, 5 to 10 minutes.

SLOW COOKER PUMPKIN

DUMP CAKE

Yield: 12 *servings* *Prep Time:* 5 *minutes* *Cook Time:* 4 *hours*

This slow cooker dump cake makes the holidays easy. While your oven is filled with the turkey, your dessert can be slowly cooking to perfection in the slow cooker—no need for extra oven space. You won't have to remember to bake dessert three days ahead of time either! The pumpkin custard-like filling cooks to a creamy, smooth consistency in the slow cooker, while the topping is sweet and crunchy. You can even add $\frac{1}{2}$ cup chopped pecans to the top for a bit of extra crunch.

Let this cake cool a little, and scoop it right out of the slow cooker to serve. Top with a little whipped cream and it's ready to go.

1 (15-ounce) can pumpkin purée

1 (12-ounce) can evaporated milk

4 large eggs, beaten

¾ cup packed light brown sugar

¾ cup granulated sugar

1 teaspoon ground cinnamon

½ teaspoon ground ginger

½ teaspoon kosher salt

¼ teaspoon ground cloves

¼ teaspoon ground nutmeg

1 box yellow cake mix

½ cup unsalted butter, melted

1. Spray the crockery insert of a 4-quart slow cooker with cooking spray.

2. Combine the pumpkin, evaporated milk, eggs, brown sugar, granulated sugar, cinnamon, ginger, salt, cloves, and nutmeg in a large mixing bowl, and stir until smooth. Pour the batter into the slow cooker.

3. Sprinkle the cake mix in an even layer over the pumpkin mixture.

4. Pour the melted butter over the cake mix.

5. Cover and cook on low for 4 hours or on high for 2 hours.

TIP: If you really love pumpkin, use a pumpkin quick bread mix in place of the yellow cake mix in this recipe as a topping for the pumpkin filling.

PUMPKIN
DUMP CAKE

Yield: 12 servings   Prep Time: 10 minutes   Bake Time: 50–60 minutes

How can you have all of the flavor of pumpkin pie without having to endure the hassle of homemade pie crust or resort to bland frozen crusts? You make a pumpkin dump cake!

Pumpkin pie filling is a classic custard-like dessert that has been a Thanksgiving standard for decades, but in this recipe, it is topped with a crumbly sweet mixture that adds texture and sweetness to the creamy pumpkin. You'll need to let this dump cake cool completely and store it in the refrigerator just as you would pumpkin pie. It will keep for a couple of days in the refrigerator if it is covered tightly. Serve this dump cake with a generous dollop of whipped cream dusted with freshly ground nutmeg. You'll never even miss the crust!

1 (29-ounce) can pumpkin purée	½ teaspoon kosher salt
1 (12-ounce) can evaporated milk	½ teaspoon ground ginger
3 large eggs, beaten	¼ teaspoon ground cloves
½ cup packed brown sugar	1 box yellow cake mix
½ cup granulated sugar	½ cup unsalted butter, melted
1 teaspoon ground cinnamon	

1. Preheat the oven to 350°F and grease a 13-by-9-inch baking pan.

2. In a large bowl, combine the pumpkin, evaporated milk, eggs, brown sugar, granulated sugar, cinnamon, salt, ginger, and cloves. Whisk until smooth and then pour into the pan.

3. Top with the cake mix.

4. Pour the melted butter over the cake mix.

5. Bake until set and the edges are light brown, 50 to 60 minutes. Cool completely and then store in the refrigerator.

> **TIP:** Do you like your pumpkin pie a little on the spicy side? Add ¼ teaspoon chipotle chile powder in step 2 to give this recipe a nice kick and a delicious smoky quality.

PUMPKIN-PECAN
DUMP CAKE

Yield: 12 servings Prep Time: 10 minutes Bake Time: 50–60 minutes

This dump cake has a wonderfully smooth pumpkin filling with just a hint of bourbon. The pumpkin mixture is topped with butter pecan cake mix and a generous helping of chopped pecans, and then drizzled with melted butter before baking. The pecans and bourbon add a unique texture and depth of flavor that is beyond description, but you can leave out the bourbon if you'd like to.

Be sure to cool this cake completely before serving—this will allow the filling to firm up and the flavors to blend. Once it's cool, serve with a big scoop of butter pecan ice cream on the side or, if you prefer, a little whipped cream on top.

1 (29-ounce) can pumpkin purée	½ teaspoon kosher salt
1 (12-ounce) can evaporated milk	½ teaspoon ground ginger
3 large eggs, beaten	¼ teaspoon ground cloves
½ cup packed brown sugar	1 box butter pecan cake mix
½ cup granulated sugar	1½ cups chopped pecans
2 tablespoons bourbon	¾ cup unsalted butter, melted
1 teaspoon ground cinnamon	

1. Preheat the oven to 350°F and grease a 13-by-9-inch baking pan.

2. In a large bowl, combine the pumpkin, evaporated milk, eggs, brown sugar, granulated sugar, bourbon, cinnamon, salt, ginger, and cloves. Whisk until smooth, and then pour into the pan.

3. Top with the cake mix.

4. Scatter the chopped pecans over the cake mix.

5. Pour the melted butter over everything.

6. Bake until set and the edges are light brown, 50 to 60 minutes. Cool completely before serving.

PECAN PIE

Yield: 12 servings Prep Time: 10 minutes Bake Time: 65 minutes

Pecan pie is achingly sweet, but it can be a little tricky to make. This dump cake is a bit more involved than some dump cakes, but the resulting cake has delicious pecan pie flavor without the hassle of actually making a pecan pie. Don't try to cut this cake like a pecan pie to serve—just let it cool a little and scoop it out, still warm, into dessert bowls. Top the cake with vanilla ice cream and a few chopped pecans before serving.

If you happen to have leftovers after serving this cake, keep them in the refrigerator, tightly covered. This dessert will keep for up to 1 week when stored properly.

1 box butter pecan cake mix

4 large eggs, divided

½ cup unsalted butter, melted

1½ cups light corn syrup

½ cup packed dark brown sugar

1 teaspoon pure vanilla extract

1½ cups chopped pecans

1. Preheat the oven to 325°F and grease a 13-by-9-inch baking pan.

2. Combine the cake mix, 1 egg, and the melted butter in a mixing bowl and whisk until smooth. Set aside ½ cup of the batter and pour the remaining batter into the baking pan.

3. Bake for 15 minutes.

4. Combine the remaining batter, the remaining 3 eggs, corn syrup, brown sugar, and vanilla in a large bowl. Whisk until smooth. Stir in the pecans.

5. Pour the mixture over the baked cake and return to the oven for 50 minutes. Cool slightly before serving.

> **TIP:** If you're feeling a little unconventional, replace ½ cup of the chopped pecans with ½ cup toasted shredded coconut. You can also try substituting yellow cake mix for the butter pecan cake mix if you don't have any on hand.

MAPLE APPLE

····················· · DUMP CAKE ····················· ·

Yield: 12 servings Prep Time: 5 minutes Bake Time: 35–40 minutes

It's funny that maple is considered an autumn flavor when it is really a spring product. It doesn't matter, though, because this flavor is delicious regardless what time of year you enjoy it. Pure maple flavor goes beautifully with pecan, pumpkins, apples, and all of your other favorite autumn flavors. In this recipe, maple syrup is mixed with apples in the bottom of the pan and then topped with butter and yellow cake mix. There is even a touch of maple sugar dusted on top of everything.

Be sure to use real maple syrup in this recipe and not maple-flavored syrup. It makes a difference in the flavor of the finished dessert. Maple syrup comes in grades A, B, and C. For baking and general use, grade B is just right.

2 (21-ounce) cans apple pie filling (or 4 pounds fresh apples, peeled, cored, and sliced)

½ cup pure maple syrup, divided

1 box yellow cake mix

1 cup unsalted butter, melted

½ cup chopped pecans

¼ cup maple sugar

1. Preheat the oven to 350°F and grease a 13-by-9-inch baking pan.

2. Spread the apple pie filling in the bottom of the pan, and stir in $\frac{1}{4}$ cup of the maple syrup.

3. Sprinkle the cake mix and pecans over the ingredients in the pan.

4. Whisk together the melted butter and the remaining $\frac{1}{4}$ cup maple syrup in a small bowl, and pour over the top of the pecans.

5. Sprinkle the maple sugar over everything.

6. Bake until set, 35 to 40 minutes.

TIP: Maple sugar is what is left after the maple syrup has all boiled out of the pot. It gives a delicious maple flavor to all kinds of foods and makes for a sweet and flavorful topping in this recipe. It is available in many grocery stores and online.

CRANBERRY

Yield: 12 servings Prep Time: 5 minutes Bake Time: 45–50 minutes

Although cranberry sauce is often thought of as a relish to be served alongside poultry, in this recipe it is used as a main ingredient to provide a tangy contrast to the sweetness of pineapple in an easy holiday dessert. White cake mix is spread on the top of the fruit to create a buttery vanilla-flavored crumble as it bakes. The resulting combination of crimson fruit and light, cakey crumble is a perfect combination for the holiday season. Serve a scoop of this cake in a pretty dessert bowl with whipped cream spooned on top—you might even sprinkle a little green-colored sugar on top of the whipped cream to make it pretty.

If you prefer, you can substitute 4 cups fresh sliced apples or a 21-ounce can apple pie filling for the pineapple in this recipe.

1 (20-ounce) can crushed pineapple
   in juice

1 (20-ounce) can whole-berry
   cranberry sauce

1 box white cake mix

½ cup unsalted butter, melted

1. Preheat the oven to 350°F and grease a 13-by-9-inch baking pan.

2. Pour the pineapple into the pan, along with the juice, and spread evenly.

3. Add the cranberry sauce evenly over the top.

4. Top with the cake mix.

5. Pour the melted butter over the cake mix.

6. Bake until set, 45 to 50 minutes.

6

Dump Cakes for Special Diets

ONE OF THE MOST difficult things about following a special diet is the fact that sweets and desserts are often the first things to be stricken from the menu. It doesn't matter whether you are vegan, gluten-free, sugar-free, fat-free, or simply trying to eat real foods and whole grains, it can be nearly impossible to find something to satisfy your sweet tooth that won't require you to break your diet. If you are having trouble finding a dessert that complies with your special diet, look no further! All you need to do is read through these recipes and pick one that works for you.

Once you've found a recipe that fits your diet, don't be afraid to create variations using different ingredients. Vary the fruit and the cake mix flavors to give yourself infinite possibilities. From Whole-Grain Spiced Cranberry-Pear Dump Cake to Three-Point Peach-Mango Dump Cake—it's all here. You'll finally be able to have your cake and eat it, too.

WHOLE-GRAIN SPICED CRANBERRY-PEAR

·········· DUMP CAKE ··········

Yield: 12 *servings Prep Time:* 5 *minutes Bake Time:* 30–35 *minutes*

Tart cranberries and sweet pears are covered with a spicy, whole-grain gingerbread topping in this delicious recipe. It is crunchy and buttery—a perfect balance to the soft fruit and sharp cranberry flavor. Serve this cake warm with a scoop of your favorite vanilla ice cream or homemade whipped cream.

Whole-grain cake mixes can be difficult to find. Although some grocery stores do carry them, you are most likely to find them at a natural foods market or health-food store. You can find these products online as well. If you prefer, you will find a recipe for homemade whole-grain cake mixes in Chapter 7.

If you are using fresh pears in this recipe, sweeten them with honey, organic sugar, date sugar, stevia, or your favorite natural sweetener.

1 (14-ounce) can whole-berry cranberry sauce

2 (15-ounce) cans sliced pears in juice, drained (or 4 cups sliced fresh pears)

1 box whole-wheat gingerbread or spice cake mix

½ cup chopped walnuts

½ cup unsalted butter, melted

1. Preheat the oven to 350°F and grease a 13-by-9-inch baking pan.
2. Spread the cranberry sauce in the bottom of the pan.
3. Cover the cranberry sauce with the pears.
4. Top with the cake mix.
5. Sprinkle the walnuts over the cake mix.
6. Pour the melted butter over everything.
7. Bake until the topping is golden, 30 to 35 minutes.

TIP: Add ¼ cup orange juice to the cranberries and pears in this recipe to add a little extra flavor and sweetness to this wholesome dessert.

WHOLE-GRAIN VEGAN CHERRY-PINEAPPLE

·········· DUMP CAKE ··········

Yield: 12 servings   Prep Time: 10 minutes   Bake Time: 35–40 minutes

When you are a vegan, it can be tough to find convenience foods that don't have animal products in them. If you have a found a vegan cake mix that you like, you can use it in this recipe. Otherwise, use the Homemade Whole-Grain Vegan Yellow Cake Mix recipe in Chapter 7.

Whole grains are full of fiber and nutrients that processed flours and grains simply don't have. They also give a rustic flavor and texture to the recipes that contain them. Whole-wheat cake mix gives this dump cake a bit of extra crunch, while the coconut oil adds a hint of tropical flavor as a delicious stand-in for butter. If you are using fresh cherries in this recipe, they can be sweetened with date sugar, stevia, organic sugar, or any vegan sweetener that you prefer. Serve this cake warm with a scoop of your favorite nondairy ice cream.

1 (15-ounce) can crushed pineapple in juice

1 (21-ounce) can vegan cherry pie filling (or 2 pounds fresh sweet cherries, pitted)

1 box vegan cake mix

1 cup shredded unsweetened coconut

½ cup chopped almonds

½ cup coconut oil, melted

1. Preheat the oven to 350°F and grease a 13-by-9-inch baking pan.

2. Pour the pineapple into the pan, along with the juice, and spread evenly.

3. Spoon the cherry pie filling over the pineapple.

4. Top with the cake mix.

5. Sprinkle the coconut and almonds over the cake mix.

6. Pour the melted coconut oil over everything.

7. Bake until the top is golden brown, 35 to 40 minutes.

GLUTEN-FREE CHOCOLATE-CHERRY
DUMP CAKE

Yield: 12 servings Prep Time: 5 minutes Bake Time: 1 hour

Chocolate and cherries are a classic combination that works well in almost everything. In this recipe, cherries are covered with a buttery, chocolaty gluten-free topping with almonds thrown in for a little crunch. Always read the ingredients on commercial pie fillings and other convenience foods, just to make sure that they haven't slipped some gluten in there somewhere. It is a good idea to read food labels every time, even if you are familiar with the product—food manufacturers can change ingredients without warning.

This dump cake is delicious served warm and topped with cherry vanilla ice cream. You can use whichever gluten-free cake mix you'd like. If you can't find a mix you like, try one of the homemade gluten-free mix recipes in Chapter 7.

1 (21-ounce) can cherry pie filling (or 2 pounds fresh sweet cherries, pitted)

1 box gluten-free chocolate cake mix

1 cup unsalted butter

1 cup chopped toasted almonds

1. Preheat the oven to 350°F and grease a 13-by-9-inch baking pan.

2. Spread the cherry pie filling in the bottom of the pan.

3. Sprinkle the cake mix over the cherries.

4. Slice the butter thinly and scatter the slices over the cake mix.

5. Sprinkle the almonds on top.

6. Bake until the top is set and the cherries are bubbling, about 1 hour.

TIP: If you do not like cherries, or if you simply want to try something different, substitute 5 or 6 cups fresh raspberries, sweetened to taste, for the cherry pie filling in this recipe.

GLUTEN-FREE PEACH

Yield: 12 servings Prep Time: 5 minutes Bake Time: 50 minutes

Gluten intolerance is becoming increasingly more common—in fact, 1 in 133 people have celiac disease or some level of gluten intolerance. The positive side to this is that it is easier than ever to find products that don't contain gluten. Gluten-free cake mixes are now available in the baking aisle of most conventional grocery stores and, since fruit doesn't have gluten anyway, you can make a simple dump cake that is delicious and gluten-free.

Use canned fruit in juice or fresh fruit when making a dump cake for a special diet or allergy. There may be gluten in some canned pie fillings, so choosing fresh fruit is the best way to avoid that possibility. No one will miss the gluten in this recipe because it is so delicious. You can swap out the peaches for any fruit you like. Serve this cake warm or at room temperature.

1 (29-ounce) can sliced peaches in juice (or 3 pounds fresh peaches, peeled, pitted, and sliced)

1 box gluten-free yellow cake mix

½ cup unsalted butter, melted

1 cup chopped pecans

1. Preheat the oven to 325°F and grease a 13-by-9-inch baking pan.
2. Pour the peaches into the pan, along with their juice, and spread evenly.
3. Sprinkle the cake mix over the peaches.
4. Pour the melted butter over the cake mix.
5. Sprinkle the pecans over everything.
6. Bake until set, about 50 minutes.

FAT-FREE ANGEL FOOD PINEAPPLE
······································· DUMP CAKE ·······································

Yield: 12 servings Prep Time: 5 minute Bake Time: 35–45 minutes

What could be more heavenly than angel food cake and sweet pine-apple? A pineapple angel food cake with zero fat! The angel food cake mix in this recipe makes this cake moist and light—it is more like a traditional cake than most other dump cakes, and it is not overly sweet. Good news for people watching their calories—without the whipped topping, this cake is very low in calories and has no fat. In fact, it is just 3 points in major weight-loss plans if you use fat-free whipped topping.

This dump cake is extremely easy to make as long as you follow the instructions carefully. There are two different kinds of angel food cake mix sold in stores—one with two bags of ingredients and another type with just one bag. This recipe works best with the type that has just one bag in the box.

1 box angel food cake mix

1 (20-ounce) can crushed pineapple in juice

1 (12-ounce) container fat-free whipped topping

1. Preheat the oven to 350°F and grease a 13-by-9-inch baking pan.

2. Combine the cake mix and pineapple in a large bowl and stir until just blended. Spread evenly in the baking pan.

3. Bake until the top is level and golden brown, 35 to 45 minutes. Cool upside down in the pan (see the following Tip).

4. Frost the cooled cake with the whipped topping.

TIP: To cool the cake upside down, place four unopened tuna fish cans on the counter, spaced so that the corners of the baking dish will rest on them. When the cake is done, carefully turn the pan over and rest the corners on the cans. Do not loosen the cake before doing this or it might fall out of the pan. Cool the cake completely before frosting.

FAT-FREE APPLE

DUMP CAKE

Yield: 12 servings Prep Time: 5 minutes Bake Time: 25–30 minutes

This cake is so easy—all it takes is opening packages and stirring the ingredients together! The cake cooks around the apple pie filling so that it comes out like your favorite apple coffee cake, except without the fat. If you like, you can vary the type of pie filling you use to create different flavor profiles. This cake is delicious with blueberry or peach pie filling as an alternative to apple pie filling.

Some people like a higher cinnamon-to-sugar ratio than called for in this recipe, while others prefer a less intense cinnamon-y flavor. Let your own tastes be your guide.

Be careful not to overbake this cake. It may not look set, but if the top is golden brown, then the cake is ready to come out of the oven.

1 box angel food cake mix	¼ cup sugar
1 (21-ounce) can apple pie filling	2 tablespoons ground cinnamon

1. Preheat the oven to 350°F and grease a 13-by-9-inch baking pan.

2. Combine the cake mix and apple pie filling in a large mixing bowl and stir well. Pour the batter into the baking dish.

3. Combine the sugar and cinnamon in a small bowl, and sprinkle over the cake.

4. Bake until the top is browned, 25 to 30 minutes. Do not overbake. Let the cake cool completely before serving.

SUGAR-FREE PEACH

DUMP CAKE

*Yield: 12 servings Prep Time: 5 minutes, plus 30 minutes resting time
Bake Time: 40–45 minutes*

If you follow a sugar-free diet you know how hard it is to find desserts that don't taste bland. Even if the dessert tastes sweet, artificial sweeteners may leave a chemical aftertaste. This dump cake has plenty of flavor from the peaches and raspberries, and it can be sweetened with any sugar-free sweetener you like. Be sure to use canned peaches in this recipe because the juice will help keep the cake moist. If you go with fresh peaches, you'll need to add about 1 cup of liquid—try water or unsweetened apple juice. If you'd like, you can substitute blueberries for the raspberries in this recipe as well.

Serve this cake warm with some sugar-free vanilla ice cream.

3 (14-ounce) cans no-sugar-added sliced peaches in juice

3 tablespoons sugar-free sweetener

1 tablespoon tapioca starch

1 cup fresh raspberries

1 box sugar-free yellow cake mix

½ cup unsalted butter, melted

1. Preheat the oven to 375°F and grease a 13-by-9-inch baking pan.

2. Pour the peach juice into a small bowl. Spoon the peaches into the pan.

3. Whisk the sweetener and tapioca starch into the peach juice. Pour the mixture over the peaches.

4. Sprinkle the raspberries on top. Let stand for 30 minutes.

5. Top with the cake mix.

6. Pour the melted butter over the cake mix.

7. Bake until the top is golden and the fruit is bubbly, 40–45 minutes.

TIP: When it comes to sugar-free sweeteners, xylitol tastes the most like sugar, has no chemical aftertaste, and is great in this recipe. For some people, however, xylitol causes intestinal discomfort. If you can't use xylitol, any other sugar-free sweetener will work as well.

SUGAR-FREE BLACKBERRY

···· DUMP CAKE ····

Yield: 12 servings Prep Time: 5 minutes Bake Time: 35–45 minutes

Fresh blackberries, still warm from the sun, are a summertime treat that has gone the way of the rotary dial phone in most areas of the country. If you are lucky, you may be able to find them at your local farmers' market; you may also find local blackberries at your favorite grocery store while they are in season. The raspberry gelatin in this recipe helps thicken and sweeten the berries during baking. The sweetener can be adjusted to your taste—the ripeness and flavor of the berries will determine how much sweetener you need. The cream soda in this recipe also adds a little sweetness and a delicate vanilla flavor.

This dish doesn't need to be topped with anything, but you can certainly serve it warm with a scoop of sugar-free vanilla ice cream if you like gilding the lily!

1 (3-ounce) package sugar-free raspberry gelatin

⅓ cup sugar-free sweetener

4 cups fresh blackberries

1 box sugar-free yellow cake mix

½ cup chopped pecans

1 cup unsalted butter, melted

1 cup sugar-free cream soda

1. Preheat the oven to 350°F and grease a 13-by-9-inch baking pan.

2. Stir together the gelatin and sweetener in a large bowl. Add the berries and toss to coat. Pour the berry mixture into the pan and spread evenly.

3. Top with the cake mix.

4. Sprinkle the pecans over the cake mix.

5. Pour the melted butter over the ingredients.

6. Slowly drizzle the cream soda over everything.

7. Bake until the top is golden, 35 to 45 minutes.

THREE-POINT LEMON-BLUEBERRY
DUMP CAKE

Yield: 16 servings Prep Time: 5 minutes Bake Time: 50 minutes

Many weight-loss programs involve counting "points" instead of calories. Rather than excluding foods from the diet, these programs encourage healthy eating habits, portion control, and moderation as a means of weight loss. Because desserts are not entirely excluded, you can still enjoy tasty treats like this dump cake. With only three ingredients, this dessert is quick and easy to throw together. Best of all, it is only three points!

Feel free to alter this recipe by substituting another type of frozen berry for the blueberries. If you choose to make changes to the recipe, try to choose an ingredient with a similar calorie count so you do not change the number of points.

2 (12-ounce) packages
frozen blueberries

1 box yellow cake mix

1 (12-ounce) can diet lemon-lime soda

1. Preheat the oven to 350°F and grease a 13-by-9-inch baking pan.

2. Pour the frozen blueberries into the pan and spread evenly.

3. Top with the cake mix.

4. Carefully pour the soda over the cake mix.

5. Cover the pan tightly with foil and bake for 25 minutes. Uncover and bake until the topping is crisp, another 25 minutes or so.

THREE-POINT PEACH-MANGO
· DUMP CAKE ·

Yield: 16 servings Prep Time: 5 minutes Bake Time: 50 minutes

This dump cake has a summery, tropical flavor that will take you on a Caribbean vacation anytime of the year. Best of all, this cake is low in both fat and calories—just three points per serving! You can certainly substitute fresh fruit if you like, but in doing so the points may change. To avoid changing the points for this recipe, use a food scale and measure 12 ounces of fresh peeled and pitted fruit for each package of frozen fruit called for in the recipe.

Using diet cream soda will give this cake a vanilla flavor, while ginger ale gives it more of a tropical, spicy flavor. Either is delicious—try it both ways and decide which you like better!

1 (12-ounce) package frozen peaches

1 (12-ounce) package frozen mangos

1 box yellow cake mix

1 (12-ounce) can diet cream soda or diet ginger ale

1. Preheat the oven to 350°F and grease a 13-by-9-inch baking pan.

2. Pour the frozen fruit into the pan and spread evenly.

3. Top with the cake mix.

4. Carefully pour the soda over the cake mix.

5. Cover the pan tightly with foil and bake for 25 minutes. Uncover and bake until the topping is crisp, another 25 minutes or so.

> **TIP:** If you'd like to save even more calories in this recipe, use a sugar-free cake mix instead of a regular one. You will save approximately 22 calories per serving.

7

Make Your Own Cake Mix

IF YOU WANT TO save money and have more control over the foods that your family eats, avoiding processed foods and making recipes from scratch is the way to go. You can easily make your own cake mixes at home using high-quality ingredients. If you are following a specialty diet, you can customize your cake mixes using ingredients that are permissible on your diet. With homemade cake mixes you know what's in them, you control it, and you save money doing it.

In this chapter you'll find recipes for conventional "just like the big brands" cake mixes as well as mixes created for special diets. You can use any of these cake mixes for any recipe in this book. Use $2\frac{1}{4}$ to $2\frac{1}{2}$ cups homemade mix for each box of commercial cake mix called for in a recipe. If you have a kitchen scale, you can measure out exactly 18.25 ounces of homemade cake mix.

If your homemade cake mix doesn't have any fat in it, you can safely store it in a tightly sealed container at room temperature for up to 3 months. If your mix does contain fat, store it in an airtight container in the freezer for up to 2 months.

HOMEMADE WHITE

······································· CAKE MIX ·······································

Yield: 5 cups cake mix, enough for 2 cakes *Prep Time: 10 minutes*

This white cake mix is pure white in color thanks to the vegetable shortening. Use $2\frac{1}{2}$ cups homemade white cake mix in any of the dump cake recipes in this book.

In order to use this cake mix for a traditional cake, measure out $2\frac{1}{4}$ cups of the cake mix and add $\frac{3}{4}$ cup warm water, 2 egg whites, and 1 teaspoon pure vanilla extract. (If you want to keep the mix white, be sure to use clear vanilla extract.) Blend the ingredients on low speed for 30 seconds to combine, and then mix on high for 2 minutes. Bake the cake in a greased pan at 350°F until a toothpick inserted in the center comes out clean, about 25 minutes.

2¾ cups cake flour	1 teaspoon baking powder
2 cups sugar	½ teaspoon baking soda
½ cup powdered buttermilk	½ cup vegetable shortening

1. Combine the dry ingredients in a large mixing bowl and stir well.

2. Transfer the dry ingredients to a food processor and add the shortening.

3. Pulse the ingredients until crumbly.

4. Store in a zipper-top plastic bag in the freezer for up to 2 months.

HOMEMADE YELLOW
CAKE MIX

Yield: 5 cups cake mix, enough for 2 cakes Prep Time: 5 minutes

This recipe yields a buttery, sweet yellow cake mix that you can use in any recipe in this book. If you are baking for a special occasion, you can add sprinkles to make it a "confetti" type cake mix.

To prepare this mix as a regular cake, measure out $2\frac{1}{2}$ cups of the cake mix and add $\frac{3}{4}$ cup warm water, 1 teaspoon pure vanilla extract, and 3 large eggs. Beat the ingredients on high speed until smooth, about 2 minutes. Bake the cake in a greased pan at 350°F until a toothpick inserted in the center comes out clean, 25 to 30 minutes.

1 cup unsalted butter

2 cups sugar

1½ cups all-purpose flour

1½ cups cake flour

½ cup nonfat dry milk powder

1 tablespoon baking powder

1 teaspoon kosher salt

1 tablespoon pure vanilla extract

1. Cut the butter into cubes and place in a food processor.

2. Add the remaining ingredients and pulse until the mixture is crumbly and well combined.

3. Store the mix in a zipper-top plastic bag in the freezer for up to 2 months.

TIP: Homemade cake mixes make great gifts. Buy a cute pantry jar, fill it with mix, print a label with instructions for use, and tie a wooden spoon to it with raffia.

HOMEMADE SPICE
······································· CAKE MIX ·······································

Yield: 5 cups cake mix, enough for 2 cakes Prep Time: 5 minutes

Homemade spice cake mix is easy because you simply start with a basic yellow cake mix and add the spices. The chipotle chile powder in this recipe enhances the other spices and gives them a little heat along with a touch of smoky flavor. If you prefer your spice cake mix to be mild, leave out the chipotle chile powder.

To prepare this mix as a regular cake, measure out $2\frac{1}{2}$ cups of the cake mix and add $\frac{3}{4}$ cup warm water, 3 large eggs, and 1 teaspoon pure vanilla extract. Beat the batter on high speed until smooth, about 2 minutes. Bake the cake in a greased pan until a toothpick inserted in the center comes out clean, 25 to 30 minutes.

1 recipe Homemade Yellow Cake Mix (page 85)

1½ teaspoons ground cinnamon

½ teaspoon ground nutmeg

¼ teaspoon ground cloves

¼ teaspoon ground ginger

⅛ teaspoon ground allspice

⅛ teaspoon chipotle chile powder, optional

1. Cut the butter from the Homemade Yellow Cake Mix recipe into cubes and place in a food processor.

2. In a large mixing bowl, combine the yellow cake mix and spices. Stir well.

3. Add the dry ingredients to the food processor, and pulse until the mixture is crumbly and well combined.

4. Store the mix in a zipper-top plastic bag in the freezer for up to 2 months.

> **TIP:** Roasted cinnamon is a more intense form of cinnamon than ground cinnamon, and it can be used in any recipe in place of regular cinnamon. It adds a deeper flavor to your dishes and is especially good in this spice cake mix.

HOMEMADE CHOCOLATE
····················· CAKE MIX ·····················

Yield: 5 cups cake mix, enough for 2 cakes Prep Time: 5 minutes

This is a deep, dark chocolate cake mix thanks to the inclusion of extra-dark cocoa powder. If you wish, you can use regular cocoa powder instead. This mixture must be kept in the freezer because of the butter, but if you'd like to store it in your pantry, you can avoid adding the butter until you are ready to bake a cake.

To bake this as a regular cake, measure out $2\frac{1}{2}$ cups of cake mix and add $\frac{3}{4}$ cup warm water, $\frac{1}{4}$ cup vegetable oil, and 3 large eggs. (If you omitted the butter from the cake mix to store it at room temperature, you will also need to add 2 tablespoons butter at this point.) Blend the batter for 1 minute on low speed and then on medium speed for 2 minutes. Bake the cake in a greased pan at 350°F until a toothpick inserted in the center comes out clean, about 30 minutes.

2 cups all-purpose flour

1¾ cups sugar

1 cup extra-dark cocoa powder

2 teaspoons baking powder

1 teaspoon baking soda

1 teaspoon kosher salt

¼ cup unsalted butter

1. Blend the dry ingredients in a food processor until well combined.

2. Cut the butter into cubes, and add them a few at a time while the processor is running.

3. Pulse the mixture until it forms a crumbly mixture.

4. Store in a zipper-top plastic bag in the freezer for up to 2 months.

HOMEMADE WHOLE-GRAIN VEGAN YELLOW
····························· CAKE MIX ·······························

Yield: 3¼ cups cake mix, enough for 1 cake **Prep Time:** *5 minutes*

This yellow cake mix is made from equal parts whole-wheat pastry flour and all-purpose flour to give it more fiber and nutrients. You can even make it with 2 cups whole-wheat pastry flour, replacing the white flour entirely. Whole-wheat pastry flour is made from soft wheat and has less gluten than the regular whole-wheat flour. It is usually ground finer and sifted to remove the chaff, which makes it ideal for use in cake mixes.

To make a traditional cake with this recipe, add 1 cup coconut oil, 1 cup nondairy milk, and 1 teaspoon pure vanilla extract to the entire recipe of cake mix. Mix well and beat on low speed until everything is well blended, about 2 minutes. Bake the cake in a greased pan at 350°F until a toothpick inserted in the center comes out clean, about 30 minutes.

1½ cups vanilla sugar or plain
    granulated sugar

1 cup all-purpose flour

1 cup whole-wheat pastry flour

4 teaspoons baking powder

1 teaspoon kosher salt

1. Mix all of the ingredients in a large bowl and stir well.

2. Store in a tightly covered container or zipper-top bag at room temperature for up to 3 months.

> **TIP:** Vanilla sugar adds extra vanilla flavor to this mix to overcome the grainy flavor of the whole-wheat flour. You can make your own vanilla sugar by adding 1 whole vanilla pod to 5 pounds of sugar and storing it in an airtight container for 1 month.

HOMEMADE WHOLE-GRAIN CHOCOLATE
CAKE MIX

Yield: 5 cups cake mix, enough for 2 cakes *Prep Time: 5 minutes*

This mix can also be made with all whole-wheat pastry flour if you prefer. This recipe yields a cake with a deep chocolate flavor with warm, nutty overtones from the whole wheat.

To bake this recipe as a regular cake, measure out $2\frac{1}{2}$ cups of the mix and add $\frac{3}{4}$ cup warm water, $\frac{1}{4}$ cup vegetable oil, 3 eggs, and $\frac{1}{4}$ cup softened unsalted butter. Blend the batter for 1 minute on low speed and then on medium speed for 2 minutes. Bake the cake in a greased pan at 350°F until a toothpick inserted in the center comes out clean, about 30 minutes.

1¾ cups sugar

1 cup all-purpose flour

1 cup whole-wheat pastry flour

1 cup unsweetened cocoa powder

2 teaspoons baking powder

1 teaspoon baking soda

½ teaspoon kosher salt

1. Mix all of the ingredients together in a large bowl and stir well.

2. Store in a tightly covered container or zipper-top bag at room temperature for up to 2 months.

HOMEMADE GLUTEN-FREE YELLOW
CAKE MIX

Yield: 3 cups cake mix, enough for 1 cake Prep Time: 5 minutes

Gluten-free cake mixes are no more difficult to make than regular cake mixes. This yellow cake mix gets extra vanilla flavor from the vanilla sugar. Use this cake mix in any of the dump cake recipes in this book. You can also use this gluten-free cake mix to create a gluten-free version of the Homemade Spice Cake Mix recipe (see page 86).

To make a regular cake using this mix, add $\frac{1}{4}$ cup vegetable oil, $\frac{3}{4}$ cup milk, 2 eggs, and 1 teaspoon pure vanilla extract to the entire recipe of cake mix. Beat the batter on medium speed for 2 minutes. Bake the cake in a greased pan at 350°F until a toothpick inserted in the center comes out clean, about 30 minutes.

1 cup fine rice flour

1 cup potato starch

1 cup vanilla sugar or
   plain granulated sugar

2 teaspoons baking powder

1 teaspoon xanthan gum

½ teaspoon kosher salt

1. Combine all of the ingredients in a large bowl and stir well.

2. Store in a tightly covered container or zipper-top bag at room temperature for up to 3 months.

HOMEMADE GLUTEN-FREE CHOCOLATE
CAKE MIX

Yield: 4 cups cake mix, enough for 1 cake *Prep Time: 5 minutes*

Adding extra-dark cocoa powder to a gluten-free flour blend yields
a dark and decadent chocolate cake. Use this cake mix to prepare a
gluten-free version of your favorite chocolate dump cakes or simply to
prepare a regular chocolate cake.

To bake this recipe as a regular cake, add $1\frac{1}{4}$ cups warm water,
$\frac{1}{2}$ cup vegetable oil, $\frac{1}{4}$ cup softened butter, and 3 large eggs to the
entire recipe of cake mix. Beat the batter on low speed for 1 minute,
and then on medium speed for 2 minutes. Bake the cake in a greased
pan at 350°F until a toothpick inserted in the center comes out clean,
about 30 minutes.

2 cups gluten-free flour blend

1¾ cups sugar

1 cup extra-dark cocoa powder

2 teaspoons baking powder

1 teaspoon baking soda

1 teaspoon kosher salt

1 teaspoon guar gum

1. Combine all of the ingredients in a large bowl and stir well.

2. Store in a tightly covered container or zipper-top bag at room
    temperature for up to 3 months.

> **TIP:** Try substituting ½ cup almond flour for ½ cup of the gluten-free flour blend in
> this recipe. This substitution will give the finished cake a delicate, nutty flavor. When
> preparing the mix as a regular cake, you can also add 1 teaspoon pure vanilla extract
> or pure almond extract.

Resources

BOOKS

Easy Dump Cake Recipes. Bandiera Books, 2013.

Minello, Grace, and Jen Trivalli. *The Dump Cake Gourmet: 25 Outrageously Delicious Dump Cake Recipes*. Grace Minello, 2014.

Wright, Wendy. *Dump Cake Cookbook: 40 Decadent Recipes*. Chef Goodies, 2014.

WEBSITES

"A History of the Cake Mix, the Invention That Redefined 'Baking.'" *Bon Appétit*. Accessed June 30, 2014. http://www.bonappetit.com/ entertaining-style/pop-culture/article/cake-mix-history

"Dump Cake." The Pioneer Woman. Accessed July 20, 2014. http://thepioneerwoman.com/cooking/2008/04/ dump-cake-a-potluckers-paradise

"FAQs: Cakes." Food Timeline. Accessed June 30, 2014. http://www.foodtimeline.org/foodcakes.html

Kelly, Denise O'Toole. "Dump It In, Bake It Up, Scoop It On." *The Daytona Beach News-Journal*. Accessed July 20, 2014. http://www.news-journalonline.com/article/20120516/ COLUMNS/305169994

"WWII Cooks Adapt to Rationing." Kaiser Permanente. Accessed July 20, 2014. http://kaiserpermanentehistory.org/tag/ dump-cake-recipe

Measurement Conversions

Volume Equivalents (Liquid)

US STANDARD	US STANDARD (OUNCES)	METRIC (APPROXIMATE)
2 tablespoons	1 fl. oz.	30 mL
¼ cup	2 fl. oz.	60 mL
½ cup	4 fl. oz.	120 mL
1 cup	8 fl. oz.	240 mL
1½ cups	12 fl. oz.	355 mL
2 cups or 1 pint	16 fl. oz.	475 mL
4 cups or 1 quart	32 fl. oz.	1 L
1 gallon	128 fl. oz.	4 L

Volume Equivalents (Dry)

US STANDARD	METRIC (APPROXIMATE)
⅛ teaspoon	0.5 mL
¼ teaspoon	1 mL
½ teaspoon	2 mL
¾ teaspoon	4 mL
1 teaspoon	5 mL
1 tablespoon	15 mL
¼ cup	59 mL
⅓ cup	79 mL
½ cup	118 mL
⅔ cup	156 mL
¾ cup	177 mL
1 cup	235 mL
2 cups or 1 pint	475 mL
3 cups	700 mL
4 cups or 1 quart	1 L
½ gallon	2 L
1 gallon	4 L

Oven Temperatures

FAHRENHEIT (F)	CELSIUS (C) (APPROXIMATE)
250	120
300	150
325	165
350	180
375	190
400	200
425	220
450	230

Weight Equivalents

US STANDARD	METRIC (APPROXIMATE)
½ ounce	15 g
1 ounce	30 g
2 ounces	60 g
4 ounces	115 g
8 ounces	225 g
12 ounces	340 g
16 ounces or 1 pound	455 g

Index

CPSIA information can be obtained
at www.ICGtesting.com
Printed in the USA
BVOW07s1324291116

R7652300001B/R76523PG468621BVX1B/1/P